The Psychology of Effective Education

Education and Learning

Dr. Sharon Campbell-Phillips

pencil

ISBN 978-93-5458-448-0
© Dr. Sharon Campbell-Phillips 2021
Published in India 2021 by Pencil

A brand of

One Point Six Technologies Pvt. Ltd.
123, Building J2, Shram Seva Premises,
Wadala Truck Terminal, Wadala (E)
Mumbai 400037, Maharashtra, INDIA
E connect@thepencilapp.com
W www.thepencilapp.com

Author biography

My name is Dr. Sharon Campbell-Phillips. I am from Trinidad and Tobago. I am very enthusiastic about community work and the development of others. I am also very passionate about conducting research and writing as it allows me the opportunity to share my knowledge with others and educate them as well as enhance and develop myself.

I am currently employed with the local government of Trinidad and Tobago where I work at the Division of Community Development. This Division is dedicated to developing communities so that persons' standard of living can be enhanced.

My writing career began when I was approached by a classmate from Bangladesh to collaborate and write professionally. I accepted the challenge and we began writing together. When I received my first publication, I was very excited and was motivated to continue writing, I am also a Doctor of Health Sciences.

CONTENTS

Preface

This book highlights the importance of effective schooling. The first rate of gaining knowledge of and teaching is the essential role of the school. This takes us to say that college is the area in which children discover ways to read and write to apprehend the arena around them, to make use of their intelligence and creativeness, to live and work in concord with others. Therefore, colleges are required to offer high fine education via keeping powerful teachers who accept as true with that 'all youngsters can research efficaciously and they can train any person to be successful. Consequently, the faculty's duty is to attract instructors who can make contributions to the teaching and learning procedure and think of the way to enhance the standard of achievement. The faculty vision which incorporates the college philosophy needs to cowl these problems of teaching and learning. each faculty have to have a policy for teaching and studying which may be constructed to emphasize; growing and keeping learning surroundings, monitoring and evaluating coaching and studying, the use of assessment for gaining knowledge of and using studying assets.

To my understanding, college students are increasingly uninterested in the conventional passive mastering procedure without a doubt because it does no longer fit their learning style. Learning style is a unique manner in which every baby research and learns. As an example, a few students need a quiet room to take a look at, others want to look at whilst being attentive to the song. This requires the teacher to apprehend and support specific styles inner schoolroom. The teacher, who insists on equal recurring for all students, will now not be capable of expanding each infant's potentials. We stay within the world of modern-day technology consisting of laptops, telephone cellular, and the internet. Therefore, the right school should pave the way to extra carrying out an active mastering method with the aid of making desirable use of contemporary technology resources. Via technology, instructors can make getting to know something exciting and amusing. As an example, the usage of the smart board internal our lessons makes students greater lively to interact within the lesson. Cutting-edge generation assets help teachers to manipulate learning now not present statistics. "The use and the control of mastering technologies are fundamental to powerful gaining knowledge of and achievement".

Arguably, exact faculty complements creativity and extends energetic learning opportunities through listening to personalizing studying, mastering patterns, and using generation. Students need to be responsible for their very own learning (discover ways to analyze). The teacher is just a facilitator or a manager. The kingdom that personalizing mastering is to help every scholar to do better via tailoring education to his or her needs, hobbies, and aptitudes. This can assist college students to be unbiased and lifelong newbies. As an example, youngsters analyze in numerous ways. Some kids analyze most from searching, some favor to pay attention, and others like to do ("visual, auditory and kinaesthetic"). To complex similarly, another instance is that during faculties we have fast novices and sluggish inexperienced persons. The short newcomers study fast whilst the slow novices will study but they need more time and obligations. This leads us to the importance of encouraging teachers to offer one-of-a-kind kinds of activities that meet their college students' wishes, and abilities.

Introduction

On the grounds that at the beginning of mankind, there has been a passion for schooling. Humans have been searching for high best education on the grounds that it's an essential human proper. Consequently, the seventh precept of the United States Declaration of the Rights of the kid which proclaimed by way of the general assembly is that: Each baby, with none exception in any respect, shall be entitled to receive schooling, which shall be free and compulsory, at least within the fundamental stages. He will be given schooling as a way to promote his popular culture and permit him, on a foundation of equal possibility, to develop his competencies, his man or woman judgment, and his experience of ethical and social duty, and to turn out to be a beneficial member of society (online).

Over the ancient sixteen years of coaching in faculties, it became discovered that Egyptian school faces many challenges that avoid reaching its number one task successfully. A few colleges lack cohesion, others are run randomly. Consequently, faculty performance and occasional level of educational attainment amongst students have emerge as a big trouble. Furthermore, the college weather is not suitable for studying in a maximum of colleges. Because of the arrival of quite a few weaknesses and threats in schools, Egyptian faculty reform has become a pressing remember. In Egypt, as an example, each school has to respond to various and big demanding situations. This might be visible as indicating at the least that the principals who lead colleges want to have the personal and expert traits which include knowledge and management abilities to fulfill those challenges. To bring about effectiveness in colleges, teachers and parents must have an energetic role in supporting training gadgets. Currently, there was a hobby inside the idea of the 'desirable school'. Studies into areas of school effectiveness have developed unexpectedly and college development is now discussed more fully. Researchers have expressed views approximately how colleges might be made extra effective. It became determined that there is a variety of factors that result in high- appearing college. While leadership personnel inclusive of the school major, heads of department, and teachers will probably play the most crucial component in improving school, there are many factors that contribute to excessive-acting school. This essay will study the important thing factors to high school effectiveness and if fulfillment is viable in each faculty. It will illustrate the questions of the college weather and growing an in shape academic surroundings in colleges, what powerful training is. It'll speak the vast and need for persevering with expert improvement (CPD) to improve the college team of workers. It's going to cover parents' involvement, assist, and have an impact on and training. Plenty of this essay might be about how faculties help to supply terrific studying and the impact of management and management on the school success.

Schools must be locations where every one of its network tastes the confidence that comes with fulfillment in some kinds of other. School to my know-how, is the region wherein we educate the heart of the scholar so that he can be a good member of the college and ultimately a great member of the society. This shows that getting ready excellent residents relies upon in large part on all people who work in colleges and their level of effectiveness. It would seem reasonable to argue that if the colleges are to improve, we want our instructors, principals, mother and father, and all people who challenge to contribute to achieving that purpose. This could be taken to mean that management internal faculties must be taken to a new stage of making sure that school will meet the needs of each scholar in terms of getting to know, attainment, and popular success. Faculty ought to demonstrate a few key standards of what makes school effective inclusive of the faculty weather, how students are gaining knowledge of, parent's involvement, instructors' relationship, and the high-quality of coaching and studying. The faculty ought to come to be an area that may be a haven for children, a place that allows shaping a society, a place wherein each toddler can achieve achievement. Ultimately, desirable faculty has the perception that everyone child can learn.

"Younger human beings grasp that the purpose of faculty isn't always to provide a schooling but to stimulate a thirst for studying, and to give it exists beyond the faculty gate". Researchers imply that effective schooling isn't just a remember of reading an eBook or only an average to replenish minds with statistics with the purpose of passing an exam, however, its fundamental goal is the boom of the scholar's persona and knowledge. It is the form of schooling that respects the entire baby and encourages him to be an unbiased philosopher, and come to be a productive member of the community. Plutarch the creek essayist said "a toddler's mind isn't always a vessel to be filled, but a fire to be kindled." therefore, schooling is a system to prepare an accountable and accurate citizen. This shows that the school has to offer such an environment that enhances students' boom. The faculty should be a studying community wherein college students can competently increase and augment themselves as people. Furthermore, college students must be responsible for their very own schooling and actively engaged in cooperative learning activities that cause them to understand a way to obtain better effects. This indicates that instructors ought to be equipped with capabilities and range their techniques of coaching which will reach as many college students as feasible within the classroom.

Effective training results in required and deliberate trade and contributes to creating a balanced personality of college students. The curriculums, therefore, need to be advanced in the direction of achieving instructional objectives both cognitive and emotional, and also to increase developments, skills, and values. It's difficult to acquire these desires without supplying or constructing an imaginative and prescient of what we hope college to be. Working without vision ends in random practice. The principles of excellence and vision manual the content material and techniques of the favored future nation of a school in its undertaking as a gaining knowledge of the institution, imaging the quality feasible conditions for students to research and for instructors to teach.

Powerful training is specifically interrelated to an imagination and prescient. Wallace, Jr. (1996) states that the vision is the start line for a movement plan to develop and observe a timetable to put the vision into practice.

School imaginative and prescient displays the lengthy-term goals for the college and identifies predicted results of performance. Hence, school imagination and prescient need to be written in a clean language and understood by means of the people of problem in faculty. Therefore, building an imaginative and prescient requires a leader who has the potential to bring together human beings of various views and agendas and facilitate the procedure of collaboration for the co-advent of a shared vision that is owned and practiced by every person involved. In other words, for the shared imagination and prescient to emerge as a reality in faculty, it is essential to have such form of major who can inspire, plan, facilitate, manual, and control. It's far sincerely crucial for colleges to apply proper assessment strategies in teaching. The traditional form of summative evaluation and grading procedures isn't always powerful sufficient to help students to be successful. Brighouse and Woods (2008) placed emphasis on the want for 'evaluation for learning' as opposed to 'assessment of mastering' to allow college students to work on their achievement and development. Evaluation for getting to know is a useful approach that brings excellence to teaching and learning. Through formative evaluation 'evaluation for getting to know students recognize their target from the start. They know wherein they are and wherein they're going. It presents non-stop feedback both it's far written and aural. Now not only does it assist college students to revise their work but it additionally teaches students self-mirrored image to music boom through having a portfolio. Assessment for getting to know brings college students within the system of evaluation to be responsible and in control in their educational mastering, achievement, and fulfillment. Nonetheless, instructors can make a distinction within the child lifestyles due to the fact they have got a greater effect on the students. To my know-how, suitable instructors are folks who listen to their students. They're on hand, to be had, approachable, enthusiastic, energetic, and excited. A proper instructor is one that offers students self-belief of their potential to gain excessive overall performance. Instructors need to be company however honest, display care and make the lesson a laugh and thrilling. This shows that teachers have to consider their practices, discover new methods to encourage their novices, make use of different studying styles, and make teaching exciting and effective. Furthermore, instructors must consider how to shape the sort of understanding that students get to maximize their fulfillment. It would be affordable to argue that each trainer should do a self-evaluation to be their very own mirrored image in their work. it is the teacher's record that tells him how he is doing in his profession.

Chapter One Eating Disorder and Learning Chapter Two Phobias and Learning Chapter Three Conducting Learners' Analysis Chapter Four Seasonal Affective Disorder Chapter Five Schizophrenia and Learning Outcomes Chapter Six Non-verbal Communication and Learning Chapter Seven Attitude, Personality and Learning Chapter Eight Academic Discourse Chapter Nine Asset-based Instruction Chapter Ten Depression and Learning

undefined chapter One

Eating Disorder and Learning

Ingesting problems have emerged as an increasing fact among these days' adolescents, and although consuming disorders are typically seen as affecting ladies, research has shown that masses of hundreds of boys experience consuming problems as nicely. Anorexia Nervosa is "characterized using a refusal to preserve a minimally regular frame weight" while Bulimia Nervosa is "characterized using repeated episodes of binge ingesting followed by using inappropriate compensatory behaviors along with self-precipitated vomiting, misuse of laxatives and excessive exercising". Factors that make anorexia and bulimia painful, which include severe worry of weight advantage and absence of shallowness, cannot be overstated. An anorexic personality kind normally consists of perfectionist, obsessive-compulsive, socially withdrawn, and depressive behaviors. Behaviors of bulimics commonly include poor impulse management, depression, and tension. Other behaviors associated with bulimia are sexual promiscuity, substance abuse, self-mutilation, and suicide. "Consuming issues want to be taken critically because they're potentially lifestyles threatening situations that affect a person's bodily, conditional, and behavioral increase and improvement, and they will lead to untimely death". Society and media play a huge position in the not possible dream of getting the correct frame. "Socializing marketers along with television and kids' books have contributed to the belief, even in young children, that appearance is extraordinarily vital". One of the socializing dealers is the Barbie doll. When Barbie become first showcased, three hundred and fifty-one dolls had been sold in the first yr. This symbolizes the effect Barbie had at the era of young women. Barbie's look meditated the US's ideals about girls and turned into used as a device for coaching femininity. Barbie becomes modeled after the "best western lady with lengthy arms and legs, a small waist, and high spherical chest". For instance, if a Barbie doll became an actual individual her measurements might be an impossible 36-18-38. Treating consuming problems soon after onset will increase the chance of a terrific prognosis for teens. School counselors are at an advantage due to the fact they work daily with the age organization in which eating problems often begin. Consequently, it's miles essential that the faculty counselor be informed of the caution signs and symptoms that permit them to perceive at-chance students and make appropriate referrals. Figuring out at-risk students can be hard. Bardick, et.al. (2004) say that there are behavioral, mental, and social caution signs that faculty counselors and others may also examine. some behavioral warning symptoms are excess consumption of low fat or healthy meals, counting calories, vegetarianism, fasting, obsessive rumination about food, skipping food or refusing to consume, fending off food in social situations, complaining of meals allergies or hypoglycemia, substance abuse, and turning into the family prepare dinner without ingesting what he or she has made.

A few psychological warning signs include perfectionism, competitiveness, a sense of over duty, emotional distress, complaint of self and others, conformity, outside the locus of control and coffee shallowness, temper swings, complaining of feeling fat, an incapacity to express feelings, and demonstration of black and white thinking. There are social caution signs as properly, thirty-five and that they consist of: isolation or withdrawal from friends and circle of relatives, avoidance of zero social or recreational activities, dieting schedules, and a choice to hide one's compulsive behaviors from own family and pals. Any other ability caution signal is decreased educational overall performance. In a current survey of over one thousand human beings with clinically identified eating problems, Reiff observed that human beings with anorexia nervosa report 90 to a hundred percent of their waking time is spent considering meals, weight, and starvation; an extra quantity of time is spent dreaming of food or having sleep disturbed via hunger and people with bulimia spend about seventy to ninety percent. Consequently, college students with eating disorders experience an incapacity to concentrate, irritability, nausea, headache, and absence of energy, which can bring about lack of motivation, lower instructional overall performance, and absenteeism. Additionally, deficiencies in vitamins, which include iron, can affect a student's reminiscence and ability to pay attention, consequently affecting a pupil's performance on checks and school work. There are several key steps that a faculty have to take as a way to discover at-danger students and to intervene effectively. The first step is to have a faculty-based total resource man or woman. This character would have the know-how of a way to confront the at-danger scholar, discuss concerns with mother and father, and make a referral. This would more than probably be the college counselor. The next step is to educate all college personnel approximately ingesting problems and the way to perceive at-chance students. The final step is to have a system that lets faculty personnel refer the at-chance pupil to the college counselor for counseling and assessment. After figuring out college students at hazard for an eating ailment, the faculty counselor must speak with the student's mother and father. Bardick et.al. (2004) endorse doing this through demonstrating assist and difficulty, expressing empathy and expertise, and telling the fact. While an ingesting disordered person is first faced about his or her circumstance, denial and resistance often are inevitable.

The school counselor ought to think about the component that these college students are ravenous themselves or binging and won't be able to appraise their situation. Also, the faculty counselor must make a referral to get the student the proper care he or she needs and deserves. The college ought to have a listing of suitable docs or facilities to which they can refer the circle of relatives in the course of these instances. Remedy alternatives encompass cognitive-behavioral remedies, psycho-academic approach, pharmacotherapy, dietary counseling, guided imagery, interpersonal therapy, family therapy, feminist remedy, group therapy, and narrative remedy. The college counselor may be a part of the remedy plan. Burdick et.al. Explain that this could be carried out by helping students reveal their day-by-day sports to balance work and leisure. The college counselor also can assist the scholar in transition into new lifestyle modifications or with extra demanding situations in lifestyles. Due to the superiority of ingesting issues amongst youth, school counselors must be privy to warning signs and the damaging consequences on student instructional success. College counselors should provide appropriate remedy alternatives.

Consuming issues (ED) are characterized using intense disturbances in consuming behavior. Anorexia nervosa (AN) and bulimia nervosa (BN) are the two maximum well-known ED that constitute a substantial source of psychiatric morbidity, and an essential public fitness concern inside the Western globe. Ingesting disorders in the route of records Anorexia nervosa isn't a brand new ailment. It is high-quality conceptualized as a clinical syndrome when you consider that an unmarried unique etiology is missing. Early nonsecular literature contains many descriptions of what turned into probable AN, and the outline of AN within the scientific literature was evident as early as the seventeenth century. Perhaps the earliest scientific file of AN turned into that of Richard Morton in 1689 which turned largely centered on the physical manifestation of the disease inclusive of the absence of fever or different signs of regarded diseases. Over the past three centuries, there were several case descriptions and theories about the etiology of AN. The current description of AN inside the subject of psychiatry and the perspectives on etiology and viable risk elements for the improvement of AN could be outlined later. Bulimia nervosa, like AN, represents a scientific syndrome with multiple elements contributing to its etiology. The term bulimia is from Greek which means "ox hunger" (derived from the Greek phrase limos which means "hunger" with the prefix you which means "bull" or "ox"), and is an ok description of the number one function of the sickness, binge consuming. Bulimia (definitely which means, episodic overeating) has been diagnosed because of antiquity, but it's miles essential to avoid jumping to the belief that overeating (bulimia) or vomiting in historical bills is equal to the sickness we now understand as bulimia nervosa.

As compared to AN, bulimia nervosa is a new and one-of-a-kind ailment that changed into diagnosed in the overdue Nineteen Seventies, however probably commenced at some uncertain period between the Forties and the Sixties. The path and outcome of AN are highly variable. in step with Russell (1997), the current "cult of thinness" has exerted effective and dangerous outcomes on young ladies and has determined the frequency, clinical form, and psychological content material of both AN and BN. some individuals with AN get better absolutely after an unmarried episode, some show off a fluctuating sample of weight benefit accompanied by way of relapse, and others experience a chronically deteriorating direction of the infection over many years. The lengthy-term final results of bulimia nervosa are fantastically poor. The route may be continual or intermittent, with durations of remission alternating with recurrences of binge eating. Disturbed eating conduct persists for as a minimum numerous years in a high percentage of health facility samples. In an examination, with greater than 10 years following the onset of ED some of the members, eleven% met full criteria for BN, 6% met full standards for AN, and a further 18.5%

met standards for consuming issues now not in any other case certain. Present-day category of consuming disorders; there has been a big change within the expertise of the psychopathology of eating problems and this has had a great effect on analysis and class. Within the research comprising the existing thesis, eating issues were classified in line with the fourth version of the Diagnostic and Statistical guide of intellectual problems. Since the system of figuring out chance elements for ingesting issues exceptionally depends on the way those problems are categorized and investigated, it's far essential to explain the diagnostic criteria and the underlying reason for choosing this diagnostic gadget in this study. The professionals and cons of this preference may also be discussed. The modern-day edition of the Diagnostic and Statistical Manual of intellectual problems divides ED into three predominant diagnoses/classes, of which AN and BN are the two most properly hooked up. The most important medical functions of AN are 1. the presence of an abnormally low frame weight of 15% below the anticipated, 2. amenorrhea (i. e., the absence of three consecutive menstrual cycles) among females, in whom the sickness predominantly occurs, and 3. disturbance in the way body weight or shape is skilled, such as the undue have an effect on of frame weight and shape on self-assessment or the denial of the seriousness of abnormally low weight.

Disordered ingesting has also turn out to be an increasing hassle, especially in the western subculture. A take a look at becoming carried out to decide a possible courting among disordered ingesting amongst college students and form of college. Previous studies allude to the possibility of personal evangelical colleges yielding greater ingesting problems than personal non-evangelical and public faculties. University students at two east coast universities had been compared on the ingesting Attitudes take a look at and a demographic questionnaire. The research indicated that the incidence of ingesting disorders isn't always considered one of a kind between personal evangelical establishments and personal non-evangelical institutions. The findings display some heritage, incidence, causes, and theoretical rationalization of ingesting problems. Eating issues four eating issues: A study of university kind and prevalence in the beyond few many years Americans have become increasingly more preoccupied with body image and a choice to be thin. TV, magazines, movies, celebrities, and the net all relay a message that girls and girls should be tall, be massively busted, have small waists, and be overly skinny. Males have dispatched messages that they must have large muscle tissue and as little fats as feasible. Kids and adults alike are bombarded with classified ads advocating rapid weight reduction even for folks that are clinically at a wholesome weight. Those chronic snapshots and messages create frame dissatisfaction and power for thinness in many individuals. According to a CBS information report weight-reduction plan pills, weight loss applications, and other form control diets have to turn out to be so popular that individuals spend thirty-five billion greenbacks a year on these products. Lamentably, lots of these diet merchandise and packages do now not yield desired effects and are steeply-priced, influencing desperate people to engage in poor ingesting behavior and probably to increase issues consisting of anorexia nervosa or bulimia nervosa. Reasons more than one research had been carried out on correlations regarding ingesting disorders. A lot of these have located familial troubles and issues of control to be relevant troubles related to anorexia and bulimia. Anorexia nervosa is "characterized through self-hunger, people voluntarily eat so little and exercising consuming issues, a lot that they threat death due to the fact their critical organs are deprived of the nourishment they need to function". In place of (or on occasion along of) right vitamins and exercise, some sense so desperate to trade their appearance that they fall captive to this disorder.

It is a bent for people with this disease to advantage a feel of feat the greater they're able to limit their weight loss program and growth their exercising. Bulimia nervosa "involves compulsive binge ingesting, wherein hundreds of calories can be fed on inside an hour or two, accompanied by using purging through either vomiting or inducing diarrhea using taking big doses of laxatives". That is just as risky as anorexia nervosa because of the severe heart and belly problems it may purpose. In a Cumhuriyet college study, researchers located that ladies scored better more often at the consuming Attitudes check (eat) and that both genders displayed low self-esteem, history of sexual or bodily abuse, and own family communique troubles. There may be no indication that context is a difficulty inside this observe; students in the college were said to have come from numerous backgrounds. Strain and perceptions approximately self-photographs such as ineffectiveness, weight dissatisfaction, and beauty are also elements discovered to be related to ingesting issues. In an examination of college freshmen, researchers found no boom in disordered eating behaviors amongst students already struggling with bulimia nervosa; but, the wide variety of students displaying ingesting problems extended ingesting disorders 6 from the beginning of the year to the stop. Maximum females on this observe did not benefit from greater weight, but felt more useless propelling "more terrible feelings approximately their weight". Although these ladies did now not enjoy big weight gain, pressure can reason one to lose or to gain weight depending on frame chemistry and a person's coping mechanisms. Some other explored motive is fear of lack of manipulating over ingesting and different factors of life. Individuals feeling as though they are dropping control will regularly motel to proscribing their diets and food consumption to gain an experience of manipulating. Researchers of an ongoing move-sectional examine of freshman and disordered eating at a few universities in western we stated, "The statistics endorse that fear of loss of manage over-consuming is a crucial a part of diagnostic criteria for bulimia nervosa, whilst worry of being fat is much less apt to distinguish among bulimic and non-bulimic women". Researchers also stated that a number of the three studies they performed, that as time multiplied the rejection of bulimia from society improved even though the range of women with signs and symptoms of bulimia stayed exceptionally comparable. The authors concluded that this will be because of a growing reputation or acceptance of consuming disorders, this ailment as a delegated lifestyle with the aid of society.

As mentioned in advance, weight and form control has come to be extensively usual and embraced in the American lifestyle, diminishing the negative stigma consuming problems once had. Emotional issues have been determined to be the principal purpose of disordered eating in a study performed among university and excessive college students. The study surveyed a big college, small commuter college, and public high schools on their consciousness and information approximately signs, definitions, and causes of consuming problems. The individuals replied that the primary causes for ingesting problems are emotional issues 83% of the time (college students validated accurate definitions of the disorder). Prevalence In a survey performed through the countrywide consuming issues affiliation related to one thousand and two students on personal and public college campuses throughout the United States, twenty percent of the students polled replied that they, at some point of their lives, have had an ingesting sickness. Fifty-five percent of college students polled claimed to understand as a minimum one person who struggled with an ingesting disorder and seventy-five percent admitted to skipping or warding off meals at the same time as dieting. Outside of America, consuming problems seem to be just as time-honored. A take a look at New Zealand university college students determined that out of folks who successfully crammed out the eat near 7% (seventy-one out of the nine hundred and fifty-one students sampled) were located to have a rating above the cutoff degree (thirty or better). For the eat, a score of much less than twenty suggests much less probability of a consuming sickness, twenty to twenty-nine suggests that the man or woman is probably to broaden an ingesting ailment, thirty or higher is indicative of a present consuming sickness. Inside the 7% scoring above thirty, twenty-one people (2.20% of general pattern) have been found to have eating problems consistent with the based clinical Interview for DSM-IV axis I problems (SCID-I). Many studies have centered in particular on anorexia nervosa or bulimia nervosa, but in doing so may also have probably omitted the poor habits and attitudes concerning food consumption, weight, and body photograph that appear most typically most of the college populace. The college years, especially freshman year, is an infamous term for weight gain for girls. As stated in advance, with the growing weight gain of the Yankee populace, there also comes a heightened cognizance of body image and the power to be thinner. In line with an examination carried out by Stanford University, the average age for onset of bulimia is among fourteen and twenty-one years of age in both scientific and non-scientific populations. This has a look at sought to determine differences between public and private excessive colleges and ingesting disorder prevalence. A public college is an institution that receives investment from the federal government, whereas a personal college is an institution that doesn't get hold of funding from the government.

According to the study, non-public colleges exhibited college students with more strain from parents and peers to perform consuming issues 9 than public faculties. A fantastic courting turned into located between the frequency of ingesting disorders and personal faculties. Theoretical explanations for the development of ingesting disorders Social Cognitive Theory Albert Bandura's social cognitive principle seems to explain the development of ingesting issues. Within the case of ingesting problems, individuals study the conduct of stay celebrity fashions. People from Hollywood, as well as fashions, are commonly underweight and considered appealing by way of the American subculture. Common residents' weight-reduction plan behaviors are vicariously bolstered each time that a movie star is praised for an underweight or surgically stronger frame. Normally normal people cross on intense diets related to purges lasting two to a few days due to the fact they consider that if they could appear to be the film stars do, then they'll additionally gain recognition and be properly preferred. Additionally, one-third of celebration members reinforce disordered eating when an anorexic or bulimic is informed that they look first-rate after losing weight. People hardly ever complement weight gain even when an individual who is underweight places on some wished pounds, but society could be very short to supplement weight loss when it is not needed. Regular punishment (direct or vicarious) is given to those barely larger than common. Merciless comments, unsightly appearances, and over-dramatized portrayals are made in the direction of those people to inspire them to shed pounds. As cited in advance, the media continuously keeps interested focused on ingesting issues 10 weight reduction. Stay fashions within the form of buddies or family who reveal a hit weight loss by using bingeing, purging, vomiting, or taking food plan drugs additionally may strengthen poor behaviors. Research has observed that the existence of ingesting issues is positively related to knowing pals with ingesting disorders. Maladaptive Cognitions; every other theoretical explanation for the improvement of eating issues is maladaptive cognitions. While individuals adopt altered cognitions and ideals that shape, weight, and body are consultants of their self-worth, then destructive ingesting attitudes regularly take control. The ability to manipulate these elements in their lives along with obtaining perfection is idealized and admired so that they might increase their non-public cost. When individuals with disordered ingesting efficiently lose weight and grasp willpower in the form of dieting, then the disease serves as reinforcement for such unfavorable behaviors. manage is at once associated with consuming issues in that people with anorexia and bulimia have an experience of much less management over their lives than the ones without eating problems.

 This lost experience of manipulating can also come from over-controlling mother and father, different circle of relatives individuals, presence of some other disease (such as despair), friends, and other policies imposed on their lives. Reflections on previous studies as discussed above, extra human beings have become obese and many of them overweight. With the upward thrust in obesity, American pop culture has to turn out to be ingesting disorders eleven increasingly more infatuated with the photo of a thin, physically suit frame for women and men. Celebrities who attain this image grow to be extra famous because the media depicts them as being the perfect fashionable example for all people. even though a couple of studies have shown that girls in their top 1920s to mid-nineteen, thirties develop eating issues most frequently, the more than one stressors related to university coursework, further to brand new independence (especially after leaving manage-oriented mother and father), provide an environment vulnerable to the development of ingesting issues. Also, the superiority of ingesting disorders seems to vary among extraordinary classes of universities (non-public, public, religiously affiliated). As many studies were conducted on the improvement of ingesting issues throughout the teenage years and middle adulthood, ways fewer have been carried out on the younger adulthood age institution. inside the have a look at cited earlier performed by using Stanford college, researchers observed that those in private excessive faculties have been extra at danger for growing eating problems than those in public high faculties. Feasible reasons for these findings are that non-public faculties have students of mother and father with higher expectations, coursework can be greater strenuous, and college coverage and policies fluctuate from the public machine (normally greater strict). This observation seeks to examine the superiority of eating issues in private universities with an evangelical doctrinal declaration to non-public universities without this form of an announcement of purpose (the ones without the inclusion of a congruent definition). An ingesting problems college that could become aware of itself as evangelical is an institution that has a declaration of reason or venture announcement congruent with the assertion: The Bible alone, and the Bible in its entirety, is the word of God written and is therefore inerrant in the autographs. God is a Trinity, Father, Son, and Holy Spirit, every an uncreated individual, one in essence, same in energy and glory (magazine of the Evangelical Theological Society, 2005 interior cowl). Students at those universities are also anticipated to comply with a handbook, along with

Christian-primarily based guidelines of conduct for interplay among students attending the evangelical university and others both on and stale-campus.

Consuming disorders can and do arise in teens, and even in younger children. But it's in the course of the university years that young humans, specifically younger women, are most at threat for developing them. The challenges of university existence, including pressure to underlying intellectual health problems, create what Dr. Alison Baker calls an "ideal hurricane" for those disorders, the maximum commonplace of which might be anorexia and bulimia.

The typhoon happens whilst the realities of university existence—multiplied workload, much less structure, and extra focus on friends—collide with anxieties, studying troubles, or bad shallowness. A younger female who was capable of control strain and lives afloat throughout the excessive school with loads of hard work and guidance from her dad and mom may find herself drowning inside the confusing, complex global of the university.

Consuming disorders broaden while the need to sense manage over a traumatic environment is channeled through food restriction, over-exercising, and a dangerous cognizance of frame weight. "University can be a time of loads of excitement and stimulation and also a variety of strain," explains Dr. Baker, a baby, and adolescent psychopharmacologist. "It asks younger those who are not but adults to behave in a very grownup manner, particularly if they're contending with intellectual infection and all at once should begin coping with it on their very own."

"The stress of a college agenda, dealing with a new social context, and handling impartial residing can cause re-emergent anxiety or, in some cases a new mental infection," explains Dr. Douglas Bunnell, medical director of the Monte Nido remedy middle in the big apple. "if you have a heavy dose of hysteria and you're in a social environment, and you're constantly exposed to the thin frame best, that's a great storm convergence of things that may force an inclined individual into a consuming ailment."

Complete-blown eating issues commonly begin among eighteen and twenty-one years of age, consistent with the countrywide eating issues affiliation (NEDA). The association estimates that among ten and twenty percent of ladies and four to ten percent of fellows in college be afflicted by a consuming ailment and rates are on the upward push.

A need to manipulate

Children who are at risk for anorexia or bulimia may have struggled with a want for management or perfectionism in day-to-day existence earlier than university, breaking down while homework wasn't perfect, or feeling terrible about themselves while sports didn't pass as deliberate. However, college life is appreciably tougher to control. It's not just the expanded workload and the disruption of an accustomed timetable. It's also an entirely new set of friends who're unpredictable, beginning with a new roommate (and that roommate's love of death metal, or overdue-night visits from her good-sized different).

And managing your food intake in university, famous for

nighttime pizza runs and all-you-can devour eating halls, is a whole new ballgame. Unscheduled, dangerous ingesting can cause troubles for every person, however, for college kids struggling with consuming problems, it could wreak havoc on self-control and self-esteem. "The liberty to eat at unique instances, a number ingesting options to be had whenever—it's no longer a good surrounding for folks who are at danger for ED," says Dr. Bunnell. This is mainly risky for college students who are liable to bulimia, he notes.

Bulimic, or binge-eating, patterns may be induced whilst students try to fail to paste to unreasonably restrictive diets, something many college's buffets eating halls and past due-night time smooth Mac make even harder. Slip-united states on a food regimen can lead to binges, which in turn bring about feelings of shame and guilt, and the cycle begins anew. Bulimia and binge ingesting sickness, says Dr. Bunnell, is greater "socially sensitive" than anorexia. "Binging and purging behaviors are tremendously at risk of social factors like those you discover in college," he says. College life is highly centered on peer interactions and students might also use others as models for dangerous conduct. If friends or roommates are engaging in an extensive weight-reduction plan, binging and purging, over-exercising, or the use of laxatives, it can be all too smooth to fall into step.

Disordered ingesting as opposed to consuming ailment

College students are acknowledged for abnormal ingesting behavior, however, it's an extended ride from attempts at dropping the freshman fifteen to a full-blown ingesting sickness. "No longer all people who are going on a food plan will broaden a proper disorder," explains Dr. Bunnell. "The difference is a function of latent vulnerabilities and genetics. There's a continuum. On the high, cease might be anorexia, bulimia, and binge eating ailment, and on the low stop you have got disordered ingesting." Disordered ingesting behavior tiers from fad dieting, or attempts at "easy" consuming with the aid of proscribing fat, dairy, or gluten, to greater extreme manifestations which include over-exercising, abusing laxatives, binging, or purging, which are serious, but don't yet meet the criteria for a consuming disease.

NEDA reviews that 35% of "every day" dieters progress to dangerous dieting, and of those, twenty to twenty-five percent develop partial or full-syndrome ingesting disorders.

An ingesting sickness is identified whilst these behaviors are sustained through the years—becoming dangerous, all-eating, and unmanageable. While looking to decide if the behavior is virtually disordered ingesting or something greater critical, Dr. Bunnell says it's critical to look at the impact they have in other areas of existence. "To what quantity do the consuming, weight, shape, body photo issues truly start to dominate? As an example making a decision no longer to go to a party due to the fact you're too worried about your weight, or you couldn't experience any seaside sports due to the fact you gained placed on washing in shape. If someone is starting to withdraw from everyday sports due to anxieties about ingesting, weight, and shape that might be cause for challenge."

Ingesting issues in college students are severe and may be existence-threatening in some instances. "There is a woeful lack of understanding approximately how extreme those disorders are," says Dr. Bunnell, mentioning the stereotype that ingesting problems stem from an overblown feel of vanity or desire to be beautiful. "Those aren't simply extreme diets, they're actual clinical illnesses.

The want for eating-disease related services on college campuses

Attending university for the primary time is both a thrilling and challenging time for plenty of teens as they learn how to navigate the adult international and balance freedom with responsibility. They may be supplied greater picks than ever before, however with this newfound freedom and responsibility comes additional pressures and stresses. As established in the 2007 tension disorders affiliation of us document, An Audit of intellectual fitness Care at U.S. colleges and Universities, the extended pressure and strain might also cause intellectual fitness issues amongst college students and an extra want for campus mental fitness services. That is also a period of development wherein disordered eating is possibly to arise, resurface or worsen for lots younger males and females. Complete-blown consuming disorders generally start between eighteen and twenty-one years of age. Out from beneath the watchful eye of mother and father and own family, consumer attitudes and behaviors can change or even come to be dangerous without all and sundry notices. Social strain to make pals, have romantic relationships, and acquire academically can result in maladaptive coping mechanisms inside the form of disordered consumption. Our modern-day cultural climate idealizing thinness and placing emphasis on weight as a number one indicator of fitness most effectively contributes to fears of gaining weight. Even though a few college students will test with weight-reduction plans and escape unscathed, thirty-five percent of "ordinary" dieters develop pathological dieting. Of these, twenty to twenty-five percent develop partial or full–syndrome ingesting issues. For the reason that eating issues are the mental illness with the very best mortality price, early detection, intervention, and treatment are extremely vital and offer an individual the best chance of recovery. assist–in search of decreases significantly whilst people aren't aware of the alternatives available to them, and another study determined that scholars who attended one–time intervention applications for NED recognition Week had higher ranges of genuine know-how of available campus sources for body image problems and consuming disordered behaviors than students who did no longer attend campus programming. That is why college counseling services and pupil wellness centers play this kind of pivotal role in offering outreach, training, assets, and help for the pupil frame. Responding to the want for sources for this age demographic and the volume of requests NEDA gets for records about campus ingesting ailment–related services, we initiated this Collegiate Survey venture to recognize the desires, cutting-edge services to be had, and capacity limitations to institutions meeting the wishes diagnosed. Survey participants (college provider–provider representatives) supplied data on consuming disorder–related programs and services, together with Campus screening and attention activities; educational programs and workshops; counseling offerings; academic lessons or programs; house lifestyles and peer marketing consultant packages; athlete offerings; and informational resources, together with articles, websites, and pamphlets.

Chapter Two

Phobias and Learning

What do you fear most, extra than anything else? Perhaps you hate spiders, or you don't like heights. Perhaps the notion of giving a category presentation makes you anxious. All people are scared of something. These fears are all normal; plenty of other humans sense the equal way which you do.

But what if spiders scared you so much that you might no longer walk out of the doors of your house? What if you had been so terrified by way of heights that you refused to even appear out your second-tale bedroom window? Might you fail a category if it intended now not having to offer an oral file? A few humans might. For them, their worry is just too intense.

People who have a selected effective worry be afflicted by a phobia. A phobia is a severe fear of a selected item, situation, or pastime mental health specialists classify a phobia as a tension disorder. Three different commonplace tension disorders are obsessive-compulsive disorder, panic ailment, and generalized tension disorder. You will examine greater about these within the first chapter.

Mental fitness experts have diagnosed masses of phobias. Phobias are classified. The first, particular phobias, center on one item, situation, or pastimes, such as germs, airplane flight, or bugs. The second one, social phobias are fears of being embarrassed in public whilst carrying out sports including speaking, ingesting, or writing. The 0.33, agoraphobia, is a worry of open, public areas together with purchasing facilities and playing fields.

Nobody is positive about what reasons a phobia. However, many psychologists consider that phobias are behaviors that have been discovered over the years. Someone learns to be afraid of something because he or she connects feelings of worry, anxiety, and tension with it. Different psychologists disagree with this principle and feature proposed different reasons.

Relying on the depth of a phobia, human beings can sometimes manipulate and even conquer them on their personal. In other instances, they need to be searching for a professional remedy to deal with their phobias. This eBook will explain a few strategies for dealing with fear yourself. it will additionally describe some not unusual styles of professional therapy.

Phobia, which is a form of tension or fear, is a fundamental human emotion usually taken into consideration to be a response to gadgets or conditions that threaten bodily safety or emotional well-being. Faculty phobia is a situational phobia observed in early life wherein the kid refuses to wait in school because of a positive overwhelming fear. Many children at some time in their faculty years may sincerely experience special kinds of fears be it tension, phobia from video games, answering a query in magnificence, or even reading out loud in front of their peers. Moreover, studies have shown that there are specific signs associated with school phobia that would range from stomachaches, nausea, fatigue, shaking, racing heartbeats, to happening frequent trips to the bathroom. children who be afflicted by faculty phobia are exposed to panic assaults mainly when the discern forces them to wait for college without even understanding that there would possibly in reality be a critical problem that wishes to be handled nicely, increasing the children's concerns and the mum or dad's frustrations even extra.

Now not most effective do children pass over domestic while being away within the faculty placing, however, they are additionally faced with a whole new world of trendy proper experiences, challenges, and pressures, be it social or academic; this unexpected exchange will absolutely depart them feeling down, tormented by separation anxiety. Moreover, they may be probably not so used to having such a lot of regulations set for them, which they'll feel scared, exhausted, or depressed.

Faculty phobia, college Avoidance, and college Refusal are terms used to describe youngsters who avoid attending school. Persistent non-attendance at faculty has been the situation of the extensive problem amongst educationalists for well over a century. Fears of the dark, birds, and so forth are socially and legally extra applicable than avoidance of school.

Simply, college phobia generates massive anxiety in both mother and father and teachers. Faculty refusal signs occur most usually on faculty days and are typically absent on weekends and at some stage in the summer season vacations. On the other hand, for the older youngsters who're new attendees in a new school, the scenario should depart them not to conform to the brand new place and surroundings, because they will not experience cozy due to the unexpected alternate in their friendships, teachers, and lecture rooms.

Faculty phobia is likewise because of the emotions of lack of confidence; an infant who's used to being at home around his/her dad and mom all day will sense threatened or torn far away from his/her liked ones. The teenager will feel so concerned and panicky that he/she will even experience worry from school buses if they needed to return home in a single. College phobia ought to be handled directly, but, if the kid is severely affected, then it's miles best to ask for professional assistance such as a referral to his/her doctor or head trainer. For those motives, it became important to have a look at this hassle and discover methods to remedy it for you to help phobic children.

-

Identifying college Phobia

Early investigations of continual nonattendance talked most effective in phrases of truancy; but, this simple view failed to explain the situation. Early pioneer studies determined proof that absolutely connected truancy with delinquency. They realized that bad parental control, intellectual dullness, temperamental instabilities, and damaged homes had been stated as important elements contributing to truancy. But; the primary man to describe a form of absence that became later most commonly known as college phobia or school refusal became Dr. Broadwin in 1932, p5: "the child is absent from college for periods varying from numerous months to a year. The absence is consistent. Always the parents know wherein the child is. He is near the mom or close to the house. The cause for the truancy is incomprehensible to the dad and mom and the college."

This classical description has nearly grown to be the very definition of school phobia. Different findings through Partridge (1939) referred to a group of children he categorized as psychoneurotic. Those children seem to differ from different truants in that they have been obedient, moderately nicely adjusted, and appreciated school. He seemed to them as victims of an emotional bond between figure and toddler. So as phrases, these kids suffer from s one-of-a-kind form of school phobia, which is particularly derived from a poor or nil dating of the dad and mom with the child. It is essential then, emotional trouble that causes absences.

The medical presentation of school Phobia

The clinical illustration of faculty phobia has been extraordinarily nicely described via Hersov in 1977: "The problem often starts with indistinct complains of faculty or reluctance to wait to progress to general refusal to go to high school or to stay in school in the face of persuasion, entreaty, recrimination, and punishment via dad and mom and pressures from instructors, family medical doctors, and training welfare officers.

The following are the best ways to tell whether or not the child is or isn't college phobic: severe difficulties in attending faculty, often amounting to extended absence, severe emotional dissatisfaction shown using such signs and symptoms as excessive fearfulness, undo tempers, distress, and so on. Staying home with the know-how of the mother and father whilst have to be at faculty at some degree of the direction of the disorder. Absence of huge anti-social ailment together with stealing, residing and wandering. Kids laid low with psychosis, gross physical contamination, allergies, truancy, and neurotic disorders aside from school phobia aren't taken into consideration suitable for investigation at the difficulty. All different elements need to be dominated out.

Peer problems, getting to know issues, depression, or overly anxious parents approximately these perceived bodily illnesses are commonplace reasons for school avoidance. Separation tension is another commonplace prognosis for school phobia but there may be different troubles, too. Faculty phobia is often a symptom of different issues. If bodily reasons have been ruled out and the behavior is persevering with, then dad and mom would possibly want to have an evaluation by a psychiatric expert. A college-phobic toddler is typically fearful of leaving domestic in general, instead of afraid of anything, especially at school. For instance, he can also revel in homesickness when staying at a pal's house. Often the primary test of a child's independence comes when he must attend school day by day. Aside from negative attendance, these youngsters typically are good college students and well-behaved at school. The mother and father are normally excellent mother and father who are conscientious and loving. Such parents are from time to time overly defensive and near, and the child finds it tough to split from them (separation tension). He may additionally lack the self-self-belief that comes from coping with lifestyles' everyday stresses without his mother and father's help.

Once in a while, a change of faculties, strict instructor, tough checks, a mastering hassle, or a bully may appear like causes of toddler's worry about going to school. However such elements can be most effective a part of the problem, and your infant should nevertheless pass to school while those issues are being resolved.

Symptoms of college nonattendance caution indicators

Children who worry faculty ship caution indicators that might be tough to ignore. Mysterious ailments that surfaced as excuses to escape faculty inside the lower grades resurface in middle college, resulting in tardiness, cut training, and unfinished homework assignments. Often a baby's ordinary living patterns, which include consuming, dozing, and faculty success, are disrupted.

Typologies of school phobia

Many human beings have tried to classify phobia; but, Coolidge, Hahn, in a take a look at twenty-one cases, provided proof of two times of school phobia that they know as "neurotic" and "characterological". The neurotic institution became usually younger ladies. The primary conflict on this institution appeared to be centered on the kid's "symbiotic tie" to the mother. The characterological institution consisted particularly of older boys who were regarded as being commonly more disturbed.

This evaluation changed into evolved through Kennedy. He protected parental characteristics and communique styles to differentiate between the two different sorts. Any other very thrilling finding become that of yuletide, Hersov, and Treseder in the eighty's; they discovered that there can be sub-sorts of faculty phobia and they outlined a crude class based on probable remedy implications.

Separation tension at the start of college access is complicated with the aid of terrible parental management, and it's far argued that in such instances some shape of in vivo (finished interior a living organism, like in a test or test) desensitization is the maximum appropriate first step. College phobia occurring in a susceptible child following a chief alternate in schooling: generally, the trouble is sparked off or began by using additional domestic-related anxieties. Systematic desensitization along with interest in practical troubles in the toddler's "physical and social environment" is probably to be the best remedy option.

Theories of college phobia

Psychoanalytic principle

It became glaringly advanced using Freud within the early 1900s and eventually modified and interpreted by others such as Klein, Arieti, Sperling, and Renik. As all of us know, Freud developed his concept of personality improvement by proposing interacting systems; the identity, ego, and super-ego. The id noted impulsive, instinctual tendencies in the persona involved with the pleasure of the fundamental emotional desires, in different phrases it mentioned the libido. Freud argued that phobias arose from the warfare of psychic electricity (libido). But, later psychoanalysts felt that aggression and dependence also performed a function in phobias.

Our instructional specialists are ready and waiting to help with any writing challenge you may have. From easy essay plans, to complete dissertations, you could guarantee we have a carrier perfectly matched to your needs.

Consistent with the psychoanalytic principle, that is the way it develops: An early, poorly resolved dependency courting among mother and toddler. Inadequate fulfillment of the mother's emotional needs, generally due to a negative marriage. A brief chance to the child's security causing a transient increase within the baby's dependency wishes. This will be defined by using Exploitation of this case by way of the mom; a comparable relationship between the mom and her personal mother. The expression of hostility to the child not best makes him greater structured, but additionally by using direct inhibition of any opportunity for the child to specific competitive or antagonistic feelings and additionally seductive behavior towards the child. furthermore, improvement of robust hostility closer to the mom, largely subconscious, and specific by exploitation of the mom's guilt toward him and also by using fears of the mom's safety cause using subconscious unfavorable desires, for this reason forcing him to be along with her to guarantee himself of her safety

The principle implied using this line of reasoning includes bringing the subconscious conflicts into open inside the context of a healing relationship. The conflicts are analyzed and an extra mature way of pleasant dependency wishes is sought. There has been superb disagreement amongst psychotherapists, but, approximately whether the mother and child should be separated or handled together and the way fast an infant needs to be made to confront reality and return to school.

Self-concept idea

Leventhal and Sills point out that some of the descriptive findings associated with school phobia do no longer appear to support an explanation primarily based solely on separation tension. They emphasize that a lot of these children maintain normal lives out of doors college hours. They proposed that the primary characteristic applicable to school phobia is the locating that:

"Those children usually over-value themselves and their achievements and then try and hold on to their unrealistic self-photograph. While this is threatened within the school scenario, they go through anxiety and retreat to any other state of affairs in which they can keep their narcissistic self-photo. This retreat may thoroughly be walking to close contact with mother."

So, in other words, Leventhal and Sills's idea is that children with a superiority complex, while put down in any manner, could keep away from going to high school and could alternatively stay in a secure environment. The treatment emphasized through self-concept theorists includes bringing the house and faculty surroundings into stability. The mother and father need to be extra sensible and her teachers more accommodating and at the equal time, the child desires to confront the fact by returning him to school as soon as feasible. The therapist intentionally precipitates a crisis by way of forcing the family to address the problem of right away returning the child to high school. The therapist makes use of this case therapeutically by assisting the parents to resist the kid's manipulative needs and win the electricity war. Anticipation and the precise making of plans are known to ensure that the parents are a hit.

Studying idea

The principles underlying behavioral remedies are derived from gaining knowledge of the concept. Studying ideas has advanced from experimental research inside the laboratory.

There theories explaining how phobic behavior is learned to compete for attention: Respondent, Conditioning, Operant Conditioning, and the two-degree idea of fear and Avoidance.

Respondent conditioning theory: Phobic seem as conditioned worry and avoidance responses to unique stimuli. Repetition of the feared scenario in affiliation with the newly created phobic stimuli will make stronger the fear and avoidance responses to the stimuli.

Operant Conditioning idea: its major principle is that conduct is stimulated through its effects. Conduct that is rewarded is in all likelihood to arise more regularly while behavior that is punished will lower in frequency. On the idea of this theory, one can argue that phobias and associated behaviors like mood; tantrums are maintained through wonderful reinforcements in the toddler's surroundings.

Two-degree theory of fear and Avoidance: advised that worry ought to motivate conduct and was not merely a conditional reaction to stimuli related to pain. He similarly argued that fear reduction has become operant praise for the avoidance of the noxious stimulus.

A wide style of behavioral techniques was advanced arising out of classical and operant paradigms as well as social gaining knowledge of theory, however, even though behavioral processes subject themselves to the instant problem of returning the kid to high school, arguments surrounding the guidance for and the timing and pacing of the go back parallel the ones in the psychodynamic camp. an increasing number of therapists appoint a mix of procedures tailored to take account of the specific range of toddler, family, and faculty-related issues that may be worried in any individual case.

Nonattendance at faculty isn't awesome, however as an alternative, it is constituted of a couple of syndromes; outstanding examples are truancy, early life phobia, and separation anxiety disorder. An exciting thing about college nonattendance syndromes is that their form and functions are modeled using the various contributions of causative factors, inclusive of genetic endowment, mind disorder, own family psychopathology, and man or woman signs. This makes school nonattendance a particularly beneficial version for the have a look at the improvement of psychopathology in early life.

This shows that the take a look at this organization of issues from socioeconomic and cultural viewpoints would provide brand new know-how of the issues and their causes, and the way cultural impacts on the improvement of the kid are mediated. Children's rejection of faculty will in flip deliver society's rejection of children. Society has an awesome position on this whole problem, considering kids will not have the ability to overcome the phobia so without problems if the society suggests rejection and disapproval.

Psychodynamic treatment of college phobia

Early treatment of school phobia turned into in large part psychoanalytically primarily based. Two studies have been in most cases carried out, the traditional psychodynamic remedy and the circle of relatives remedy.

Conventional Psychodynamic studies, these studies are interpreted as those focusing treatment on the person child or the mother-toddler dating. The analytic treatment became centered completely on the kid, however, they realized the significance of treating each the mom and toddler. remedy with admire to the father turned into felt to be most correctly dealt with using supporting the mom make clear and restructure her feelings approximately her husband rather than handling the father directly. The catch situation on this look at is whether the child should or shouldn't go back to high school at once. Studies showed a moderate distinction in possibilities while it got here to determine which method was extra effective, subsequently, it remains unsure.

Circle of relatives therapy (via Skynner)

Those procedures transcend the determine-infant dyad in addressing the entire family device. School phobia is appeared as symptomatic and every so often defensive of faulty own family functioning. Remedy techniques consistently emphasize the significance of early go back to high school even though the way by way of which this is executed varies substantially from therapist to therapist.

Skinner refers to his method as conjoint his own family psychotherapy. The relevant hassle within school phobia is visible because the "mother and father" failure to assist their toddler relinquishes omnipotent needs for specific ownership of the mother. Skinner argues that faculty phobic children are covered from the challenges of fact through their moms. Skynner claims that bonds inside these households run vertically from discerning to an infant with a consequent susceptible relationship among spouses.

The principal elements are pressured in this treatment: The complete nuclear family is protected in treatments in addition to other own family members in which vital. An emphasis is located upon non-verbal communique and disagreement of the parents over the hidden rule device. Attention is directed to the "here and now" of own family interactions even though past events can be taken into consideration as and once they rise up

There's a focal point on an early go back to high school. An effort is made to weaken the mother-child bond and toughen the marital bond. Within the greater trustworthy instances, interpretation of the trouble develops perception in mother and father allowing the own family to marshal its very own resources and clear up the problem. Skynner advocates the use of drugs to assist inside the disagreement level. Further, excessively timid pupils are helped through attendance at psychotherapy groups. Simplest minimum attention is paid to high school elements

Skynner feels that school phobia is exceptionally understood as psychosocial trouble rather than merely medical intra-psychic or even intra-familial disease. It's interesting to notice that the early traditional examine emphasize the significance of the conformation of the scary conditions; but, the later studies favored immediate, even forced, return to school.

Behavioral methods and treatment of school phobia

The behavioral processes are divided into three: remedy primarily based on classical conditioning, remedy primarily based on operant conditioning paradigm, and treatment based on social skills schooling.

Systematic Desensitization: This method includes operating the child via cautiously graded worry hierarchy beginning with the least feared situations, constructing up to maximum feared situations. At every stage, the kid is helped overcome any tension by using concentrating on conduct this is hostile to the tension.

Emotive Imagery: it's miles a technique that a few behavior therapists have observed to be very powerful. They use normal rest approaches in conjunction with systematic desensitization. In this approach, the therapist develops imagined scenes that conjure up feelings of excitement, self-announcement, and standard "nice impact" as approaches to inhibiting anxiety.

Flooding or implosion: these approaches involve immediate disagreement of the maximally feared situation without any cautious instruction through graded exposure to less threatening situations. The situation is maintained in the acute feared state of affairs till the tension shows visible signs and symptoms of waning on the classical extinction version. The idea right here is that the situation feels anxiety because of previous classical conditioning the bright presentation of the circumstance stimuli and the absence of any primary unconditioned stimuli will finally lead to the extinction of the tension reaction.

Operant-based remedy techniques are concerned with changing the reinforcement contingencies affecting an individual's behavior. It entails maximizing the incentives for being in faculty using constructing into the college program more effective reinforcement and minimizing incentives for last at domestic at some point of the college day by using removing tremendous reinforcement (like extra personal freedom, more personal attention):

This treatment is primarily based on reinforcement. Natural reinforcement is brought in the individual's existence in the desire to the advent of greater artificial reinforcement like candies. However, in positive cases, tangible reinforcements can be essential in the early stages of the treatment software.

Many youngsters who be afflicted by faculty phobia have essential issues in relationships with bodes language and posture. it is real that many children may additionally want to shelter from ridicule however others want help in enhancing their bodily capabilities. This treatment includes an interest in lots of regions along with frame posture mainly the challenge's stiffness and absence of mobility in the trunk and limbs.

Getting schooling can be hard for people who are susceptible to immoderate fear and tension. The cause of this newsletter is to in brief evaluate how signs and symptoms of hysteria problems can create issues for students of every age which include youngsters, adolescents, and adults. It's far vital that affected individuals and households can understand how anxiety is interfering with meeting instructional dreams so that you can take appropriate motion. Otherwise, unmanaged symptoms of excessive tension can restrict a pupil's potential to attain their full capacity.

Going to high school or being inside the lecture room can be a hassle for a few college students. Both children and adults can refuse to move to school or enter the schoolroom for a variety of motives. A few fear being aside from cherished ones or doing something on their own. individuals laid low with panic assault signs and symptoms may additionally have issues due to fear of something terrible taking place if they were to have a panic assault even as in magnificence (e.g., dropping control, embarrassing themselves, or now not being capable of getaway). A few individuals with obsessive-compulsive ailment (OCD) may additionally have a problem being in the lecture room because of obsessional issues (e.g., worry of being infected; the worry of by chance harming others; the worry of certain people, colors, or items). Different people with excessive fear or social tension may also discover it tough because of worry of being watched or judged negatively by other students or the teacher.

Giving shows or speaking out in elegance is some other very commonplace cause for those laid low with tension; for some, it's miles worry of experiencing signs of anxiety or panic while talking in front of others (e.g., trembling or shaking, trouble respiratory); for others, it is the worry of announcing the wrong issue, looking silly or doing something else embarrassing. a few people can have trouble completing their schooling or obtaining good marks due to the fact they do everything they could to keep away from giving displays or speaking out in elegance.

Taking exams or assessments is unavoidable whilst getting schooling and a few diplomae of test-taking tension is normal and expected for most of us. But, for some people, excessive tension interferes with efficaciously completing oral or written checks. Regularly this anxiety starts for the duration of the weeks and days leading as much as the examination (anticipatory tension). People with panic attack symptoms may also worry about having these signs and symptoms throughout the exam. People vulnerable to immoderate worry or social tension might also fear failure or no longer assembly personal standards. Individuals who have perfectionistic standards can be particularly susceptible to immoderate overall performance tension during checks or other academic activities (e.g., excessive worry of no longer getting an A or making a mistake).

Studying cloth for a class also can be disrupted with the aid of signs and symptoms of an anxiety disorder. Many individuals with anxiety symptoms experience trouble concentrating, which could make it hard to analyze and memorize cloth (e.g., looking to examine a page after which understanding you don't recollect most of what you just read). The want to reread or rewrite what happens in OCD can appreciably prolong examine instances. Different compulsions or rituals also can interfere (e.g., needing tissue to turn pages, turning a web page on a superb notion, etc.). it could additionally be difficult to make selections while tormented by tension and this indecision can intrude with efficaciously completing educational assignments.

Other barriers related to immoderate tension within the educational putting include problems with powerful time control, transportation to school (e.g., worry of riding or taking the bus), using public resources which include the washroom or library, and talking with instructors or professors. approximately fifty percent of individuals with a tension disease also revel in symptoms of depression together with issues with appetite, sleep, fatigue, or motivation, which can make getting training even greater difficult.

It can be very tempting to keep away from or end college when coping with poorly controlled anxiety signs and symptoms, however, this generally increases tension signs and symptoms and lowers self-esteem. If you or a loved one has an identified tension ailment, it's miles continually really worth exploring the available alternatives. Many colleges, faculties, and universities are capable of offering special preparations through the scholarly useful resource center or disability workplace inclusive of extra time for assessments or taking exams in a personal room. These arrangements are usually carried out sensitively and exclusively that protect the privacy of the scholar whilst maximizing their capacity to examine and complete their coursework. Preferably, such arrangements are one part of an evidence-based treatment plan along with medicinal drugs or cognitive-behavioral treatment that regularly assists the man or woman in overcoming their anxiety problems.

Chapter Three

Conducting Learners' Analysis

A learner's evaluation is a report this is important to reap facts approximately a target audience this is created by the instructional clothier. A written record containing everything that desires to be regarded about the audience ought to be documented. The learner evaluation will assist observe the space between college students' current abilities and know-how and what is necessary for them to learn that allows you to acquire educational goals and objectives. In designing training, the learner and desires evaluation are essential steps. The goals should be of essential purpose of finishing a learner evaluation are who's the meant target market for the training, what is the motivation for collaborating within the instructional occasion? and the way has the instructional clothier deliberate for the accommodation of culturally and physically numerous newcomers? Who's the meant target market for the guidance? Newbies evaluation is the manner of identifying who your target market is, earlier know-how, their demographics, physiological and affective, and social needs. Every one of the point-out attributes will form the design selections and have an impact on the educational model or techniques and techniques that can be implemented. While instructors are designing educational opportunities, the designers usually assume that everyone learns the same way she or he does. For software to be very effective it ought to be stimulating to the central target audience; if that is so, how then can this be done? Building the profile of the target audience using a questionnaire may be a treasured location to start. Parrish (2019) posited that "the key to the educational design is to work across the participants in place of the contents. There has to be a deliberate attempt to be sensible; the target market often involves the dressmaker with a huge form of pastimes and expertise. This system fashion designer may appear careworn and beaten, but with open-mindedness, careful preparation, a successful project can result. The reason of the target audience is to analyze the traits of the learner that is anticipated to be used within the practice. An analytical overview that is ideal for the target market frequently helps the clothier in designing instructions this is powerful and exciting to the learner. The project or problem associated with this intention may be unrealistic feedback from the target market. What is the motivation for taking part in the educational event? Enhancing student motivation in an academic event is one of the most important demanding situations instructors often have inside the schoolroom. Commonly, there is forms of motivation, intrinsic and extrinsic motivation. Intrinsic motivation takes place in which a pupil already has developed an interest in gaining knowledge of the difficulty and has an interior notion. Extrinsic motivation, however, takes place while different elements inclusive of recognition, pressure to participate in elegance, and praise.

The duty of riding both intrinsic and extrinsic motivation

relaxation with the instructor to drive a) whilst an instructor fosters a fantastic learning environment: It motivates the students to research. A trainer's persona sets the tone for the lecture room. "While you show enthusiasm and ardor for the situation you're coaching, it can be contagious for maximum college students, who will version your positive conduct. Except coaching the curriculum, is a function version to boost positive actions to motivate college students to analyze. Make sure that study room policies are distinctive, so students feel secure to participate and proportion their reviews and remarks without ridicule. When there's a positive courting among trainer and pupil, there could be greater engagement in getting to know. Institution discussion must be about topics that interest them; this can assist find their personalities. "Supply surveys with questions on their favored books, films, hobbies, and sports activities. Speak in confidence to your college students as well about your background and hobbies to expose you are without a doubt interested in making connections". Prepare an engaging lesson: amusing a thrilling fabric is usually essential for college kids; a trainer should find a manner to facilitate activities that provide perception to their historical past, interest, and destiny goals. "Snatch their attention with stimulating music, artwork, and hands-on sports to tune them into the curriculum. For instance, if you are turning in a lesson on poetry, play a modern song and discuss poetic devices inside the lyrics rather than just studying poems. Use technology to liven up study room sports". begin a reward gadget: profitable college students have regularly validated to be a reinforcer of superb behavior in students, and this often ends in the internalization of the choice to study. A praise application may be praising students after they complete an assignment or an undertaking or active members at some stage in group discussion. The undertaking or problem related to this goal can be a time constraint. How has the instructional dressmaker planned for the lodging of culturally and bodily diverse inexperienced persons? For my part, the third maximum crucial attribute is how the educational fashion designer plan to accommodate culturally and bodily diverse freshmen. A conventional layout for studying (UDL) framework is used to support diverse beginners. Everyday layout for learning (UDL) may be running Head: desires of finishing novices' analysis prolonged to seize how studying is influenced with the aid of cultural variability and show how the UDL framework is probably used to create a curriculum that is aware of this cultural size of learning. Provide picks to sustain scholar engagement: allow students to select an activity. For guided practice, they might determine whether to reply to questions independently and acquire comments, play a recreation, do a function play, or exercise in a group.

To illustrate their expertise of an idea, they might determine whether or not to create a poster or assemble a model, write a paper, make a video or podcast, or do a presentation. Making alternatives allows them to narrate the content material in a way that sparks their interest. Offer resorts for all students: as opposed to imparting motels simplest to students with an IEP or a plan, reflect on consideration on resorts that such college students often need and make them available to all students. For instance, if you frequently have students who need a replica of the notes, the use of a domain like Blackboard or

Google lecture room to publish every slide presentation and task makes it easier for all of us to get admission to those substances. The challenge or hassle associated with this aim can be a lack of enough time and space. In growing effective instructional materials, learners' fashion may be very crucial. The educational clothier should be able to pick out his target market. Wynne (2013), identified categories of inexperienced persons' characteristics: physiological, cognitive, affective, and social. Considering the precise earlier expertise of the learner's population is thought to be the most vital learner trait to take into account within the instructional layout evaluation.

Understanding your ingredients earlier than you start cooking the dish is as important as understanding your novices earlier than starting with the teaching manner. Carrying out a learner evaluation is essential due to the fact of having sound knowledge of who the beginners are, what they already realize, what way of life they belong to, and so forth. Enables the instructor to satisfactorily deal with their needs in their article, provide a listing of desires that assist in guiding an instructor when they want to finish a learner analysis. All the nine dreams are vital, however, three of them hold more importance to the writer. Every one of them may be elaborated on, justifying its significance, together with providing a venture to it. Who is the intended target audience for the guidance? This crucial question that every instructor ought to ask earlier than even making plans the instruction has lots of details connected to it. By using asking and studying who the learner is, the teacher can get statistics that could change not handiest the planning but even the curriculum.

As an instance, a private excessive school would possibly want to understand the level of English of students before signing them in. consistent with their scalability in English, they might be given extra lessons earlier than getting started with all the different subjects. That is only a simple example of why knowing your inexperienced persons' profile is essential in determining the dreams and targets of learning and making plans the education for that reason. However, the facts gathered won't constantly lead the trainer to the best selection. For instance, an unmarried exam won't honestly display the level of a pupil for his or her English proficiency. From a pupil that has spent a sleepless night time from being unwell and doesn't do his exceptional to a scholar that is simply lucky sufficient and selects the right answers using risk, some possibilities can lie to the undertaking A learner analysis. In one of these cases, it might bring about a student taking remedial English instructions without needing them, and another student having difficulty courses and suffering due to the dearth of his English stage. This is only a dilemma of this goal, and it doesn't function as a disadvantage for the teachers now not to investigate their learners. What's the range of capability of some of the rookies? Even in this component, we are following the equal point, knowing who our college students are. However, this time, we are considering their talents and the way that varies. The variety of students inside the schoolroom may be very rich. This means the instructor may input a lecture room, which has twenty different characters and abilities, with a unified lesson plan. If so, maximum in all likelihood, the coaching may only deal with the desires of a few rookies, but now not all. This is why understanding the variety of capacities of your audience is essential in making plans powerful guidance. If the instructor plans sports and responsibilities that range from easy to tough, it might be possible that all students get engaged and concerned within the lesson at a higher charge than they could with unified-stage sports. A problem with this goal is the war that the trainer has whilst locating suitable activities for all of the abilities inside the elegance. It might not usually be the very best element to break the principle concept of a topic into degrees and abilities, considering the diversity of students in a class. Do the learners' have non-academic needs (e.g., rest, food, protection) that should be met so that they will recognize in the educational pastime? The final question to be taken into consideration is whether or not inexperienced persons produce other non-academic needs that must be met. That is certainly replied as 'sure.' One aspect of this is considering students' power and awareness while planning a timetable. As an example, subjects like Math and conducting a learner's analysis three science tend to be placed at the beginning of the day; in the meantime, Arts and PE are probably scheduled for the last sessions of the day.

This happens because it's clear that by way of the end of the day, students are extra tired and cannot attend as well as within the beginning. Every other detail related to that is ensuring the study room is a secure surrounding for all people. Some college students' desks might be located right underneath the air condition and might be afflicted by too much cold or warm; meanwhile, for the relaxation, the temperature is exceptional. The trainer has to attempt to make it as truthful as viable by giving anyone the same possibilities. in addition to this, when the students have been in magnificence for three to four or maybe five hours directly, they truly may need a short physical pastime intervention. Regardless of what the subject is, the teacher may have all and sundry just move around the elegance and search for items that might be associated with the subject of the lesson for that day. This is only a bad instance, possibly, however, the college students would get the possibility to move and stretch their muscle tissues, which helps in better concentration. "Motion is one of the great approaches for youngsters and teens to benefit manage over their conduct, have interaction of their getting to know, and hold what they're being taught. Sitting for long intervals of time definitely works in opposition to the capability of students to research efficiently. Many mother and father and teachers are actually figuring out that incorporating exercise and movement into the study room better prepares the body to research". What approximately while a scholar is hungry, and there's no longer much a trainer can do about it at that second? Nicely, this appears to be a difficulty for this aim. The teacher can nearly continually deal with their needs, but can't reach them all. While the students have lunch bins, the instructor may permit a hungry one to consume a bite or two, however, this might cause many others to need it as nicely. generally, I've experienced college students soliciting for the restroom best due to the fact a person else becomes undertaking a learner's evaluation. Simply granted a go to the bathroom. The instructor trying to reach all their desires may often develop into frustration and chaos. To sum up, there are numerous goals in seeking to conduct a learner analysis as an instructor and all the steps are crucial. A few are more than the relaxation, so three of them were taken under consideration and analyzed along with a problem for every.

Ritchard (2015) mentions five beliefs that encourage putting high expectations on college students. These action theories consistent with him can facilitate a culture of thinking or act as an inhibiting task to the development. Cognizance right here shall be on any such challenges – growing a growth as opposed to a set mindset. Mind-set refers to how someone views, "shape the way one procedure getting to know possibilities". The growth mindset believes that mastering grows with time and experience. Studying isn't a hard and fast asset. Failure isn't always the realization of the problem but an opportunity to reflect on what happened and bounces returned. The boom attitude is prepared to stand demanding situations and obstacles even though they may or might not be triumphant. Existence is constantly a getting-to-know procedure and challenges a possibility to develop. The lowest line here isn't always giving up however maintains trying.

The fixed mindset, on the other hand, might either take delivery of fulfillment or not anything. Right here there may be infrequently room for a second hazard. College students in this example will easily get annoyed and surrender. The venture is not a part of them. The second hazard isn't always very a good deal in their vocabulary. College students will handiest want to paste to that which they realize or are used to. They're not bendy of their questioning method. Consistent with Dweck (2007), such individuals are much more likely to surrender whilst faced with difficulties and to judge their overall performance harshly. As Ritchart (2015) places it, they shrink back from possibilities to research new matters and increase their skills out of fear that failure will divulge them as no longer being as smart or talented as others may think they are. In the face of these mindsets, what moves can instructors use to promote academic merit and positive schoolroom surroundings?

Teachers have the obligation of supporting college students to broaden their growth mindset. With the aid of giving high-quality feedbacks to college, students feel inspired to study. Consistent with the college of studying "feedback is a critical a part of powerful gaining knowledge of. It allows students understand the situation being studied and gives them clear steerage on how to improve their learning." comments have to be such that it may construct self-assurance in the pupil. Ritchart (2015) says remarks like "That changed into absolutely hard, however you caught to it and completed something" is greater profitable than truly announcing "correct process!" Even the ones in standard usually feel satisfied whilst given verbal or non-verbal comments for being a great line chief or certainly demonstrating proper behavior. This gives them clear steering to recognize they're following the rules or are on the right music.

Instructors also can use special techniques in dispersing their lessons. The use of different strategies can assist to construct specific mastering skills to vary the content of the lesson. The trainer should make the lesson plan to be greater engaging. There will be changes in the content, the manner, and the product. Added to this, students might be concerned about making plans for the lesson. one-of-a-kind sports, getting to know stations, learning facilities, audiobooks, puzzles, and another era will be used to make the lesson greater attractive. The think-pair-percentage strategy can also be used to encourage their mastering. A pupil will also be advocated to study exclusive genres of books apart from the ones they may be used to. College students must be advocated to invite for clarifications, supply guidelines, and get comments getting to know is a continuous technique, and instructors have to encourage students to have a positive mindset.

Online schooling and newcomers' traits

Online schooling is a progressively growing phenomenon in higher schooling nowadays; online guides and applications presented by colleges and universities have elevated by about fifty-five percent, thus distance training and related studies have proliferated. studies in this location have centered on educational layout, interplay, and their impact on pupils gaining knowledge of. The impact of beginners' traits is a critical region of this study. It's often suggested to "understand your target audience" earlier than coaching, and this is in particular crucial and essential in online courses to train extra efficaciously. Previous distance education research shows that sure learning characteristics which include personality, demography, motivation, and past experiences can account for the achievement of beginners in online studying. Therefore teachers need to recognize extra differences in beginners and the way to correctly layout and deliver training to their college students. In this regard, online schooling might also function as a possible choice to fulfill the precise studying desires of beginners. Regardless of the wealth of studies literature on distance training, drop-out prices are very high. To provide an explanation for and save you pupil drop-out, it is important to study no longer simplest gaining knowledge of effects and success, however additionally the predictors of student pride. The pleasure from distance education; as preceding studies have proven, distance learners' pleasure has an impact on their selection approximately whether or not to drop out or persist. Pride can be depending on external factors such as motivation, interplay with instructors and different students, support offerings, path materials, and learner traits. Knowledge student characteristics can also help predict pleasure from distance schooling. Moreover spotting the traits of the target market in designing powerful preparation may additionally grow distance learners' delight from the studying revel. furthermore, high-quality mastering can be evaluated by way of assessing newbies' pleasure. Several research has indicated the significance of delight of learners gaining knowledge of style and preference for traditional (e.g., classroom) and online guidance.

Understanding the size and demographic of your learner population enables you to design a route that best addresses their variety of needs. as an example, the varieties of interactions within the route and the extent of comments you could provide will vary, relying on whether it's far a big magnificence that is required for a main with hundreds of newcomers or a graduate-stage seminar with only a few. Additionally, person learner profiles should inform your path design.
The issues indexed underneath are important when you are

considering your beginners and determining what sort of route design, content material, and transport technique will assist them to develop. Being able to answer those questions in addition to apprehend the reasoning behind them is vital to simply connect for your novices and growing an effective online environment for them.

Factors to recollect approximately the newcomers

What's motivating rookies to take this direction? Are newbies taking my path to earn a diploma or extend their professional abilities in this subject region? Do my beginners have any professional experience? Knowledge of the specific characteristics of your freshmen will help you lay out a route to leverage their intrinsic motivations. Moreover, identifying characteristics of a cohort or group can provide additional opportunities to interact with your learners on that common ground. As an instance, a government MBA program can also anticipate freshmen with some diploma of professional enjoy, while freshmen in an undergraduate course won't have any relevant work history.

What do my learners already understand? Are learners acquainted with the challenge rely on?

Have the inexperienced persons completed the proper prerequisite coursework? Do the newcomers have the generation abilities important to complete assignments? Having a concept of your freshmen' expertise base will assist you in awareness of your educational dreams. In this manner, you do not spend precious time reviewing fabric that they already know or count on them to be successful with concepts for which they do now not yet have sufficient foundation.

Multicultural considerations:

Wherein are my learners coming from?

Do any examples require precise cultural understanding? (e.g., baseball or cruising). Do the newcomers have language boundaries? Is the content material culturally sensitive? The rationale of education is to communicate with the freshmen, so it's miles vital to be aware of any cultural factors which can hinder or adversely impact the drift of data. In internet surroundings, that is mainly essential because you can't examine body language or make eye touch with the rookies. Get entry to technology: How does get entry to digital and net equipment affect the freshmen? How does get entry to digital and net equipment impact the novices? How will novices get entry to your direction? (e.g., laptop lab or private devices). Do the learners have to get admission to all system important to finish assignments? (e.g., video digicam or software). Are your substances universally reachable? (e.g., mobile-pleasant, closed captioned, significant link titles, and many others.)

As an educator, you want to be sure that every one of your newbies has the gear they need to be successful. If the content is developed and shared digitally, it's first-class to lay out with these issues in mind so that you ought no longer to retrofit the content material. You should broaden flexible content that may be presented and fed on across diverse gadgets so that you do now not exclude freshmen with confined technology alternatives.

The significance of Learner evaluation and the way to measure it: The L&D angle

As L&D's, what is it that you genuinely cognizance on if not expertise your learner's motivation to access and sign up themselves in training and proceeding to finish it? If you have not guessed it yet, permit me to make this simpler; learner evaluation and behavioral deciphering are what you recognition on!

How are you going to virtually measure the importance of learner analysis? As an L&D, corporate teacher, or HR, what is it that your attention needs to definitely be on? Is focusing on the profitability of your company a number one task? In this example, earnings are genuinely essential, but it is secondary given that your task is to make certain human capital improvements, and that results in profits. Which brings us to the question; what usually aids human capital improvement? It is thru your ability to apprehend beginners' conduct patterns and pleasant-tuning the schooling technique that you could broaden your employer's human capital.

Why Is Learner evaluation crucial? As L&D specialists, it's time to take a scientific approach in the direction of training in comparison to ad hoc schooling practices that don't yield high-quality effects. After all, isn't that what an L&D team absolutely has to do? To recognize the underlying conduct of newbies and pleasant music it? How else can you scientifically apprehend what your learners like and nice song if it isn't for learner evaluation and behavioral studies? Learner evaluation at an agency-wide degree is crucial, and gathering the records to perform the analysis is what aids in the improvement of human capital. Those are a number of the most essential matters an L&D has to awareness of, and the solutions needed to solve corporation-wide questions will arise from right here.

Within the discipline of learner conduct analysis, humans have long gone as far as to apprehend what time of the day maximum of their employees get entry to the LMS! Is it inside the mornings? Is it within the afternoons? Do they even get the right of entry to it in any respect? Knowing the solutions to such questions facilitates growing a scientific approach to schooling. It isn't adverted hot anymore, and the statistics used are real and reliable, permitting you to method the hassle with the most possibility of achievement. Isn't that better than shooting within the dark?

2019 should be about the yr of clinical methods, and as L&D experts whose primary cognizance is to make certain worker development, expertise your freshmen could be very important. Bringing us to the next part of the hassle; how do you collect the wanted facts? Accumulating these statistics, the usage of conventional practices, requires immoderate efforts and determination, mainly, while the identical can be achieved in a far easier manner with much less time and effort worried, leaving the L&D team with greater time and capacity to plan solutions.

Fortuitously, the eLearning space has always strived to push forward the limits of progression. As L&D professionals, there is numerous gear at your disposal. From getting to know control structures with an xAPI to shrewd tutoring structures with the attention-monitoring feature, there may be a myriad of equipment available. In most cases (90%), the information needed is easy. An LMS with xAPI or eye-tracking isn't always even wanted. To the sort of fundamental degree, even a modern-day LMS can remedy most of your L&D woes, as long as it has the capacity to the song and gets better the data you want. And what facts do you really want? Again, in most instances, it's far as simple as:

- Crowning glory costs of courses and which of them they are.
- Who the maximum pro-active rookies for your business enterprise are.
- What your learners want to research.
- Why they want to study it.
- In which they're facing difficulties.
- What their strengths and weaknesses are.
- Who the excellent suit is for a sure challenge.

With getting entry to such information and the potential to automate schooling, your capacity to attain out and have interaction with learners increases. Shooting within the darkish will become a component of the beyond. Selections are knowledgeable and properly deliberate; they may be based on dependable information. Your schooling begins witnessing elevated fulfillment and inexperienced persons are inspired to educate as nicely. Moreover, these gear are simplest being improved with time to resource your characteristic of being an L&D professional, a company trainer, or a person with the responsibility of improving human capital improvement, something your position is.

However, a few L&D professionals still do now not well known the importance of learner evaluation. In a time wherein consumer purchase selections and presidential elections are won based on analysis and first-class-tuning of the human psyche the use of information, learner evaluation is vital. Consider studying and development as an investment closer to enhancing human aid, and you are in fee of it. Accumulating facts at the inner customers of an agency is as critical as gathering statistics about your clients.

The L&D procedure isn't as truthful as some of the alternative enterprise-wide capabilities like income, operations, finance, HR, and so on. The L&D characteristic needs to be performed with absolute precision, understanding, and cause. While you communicate approximately the L&D branch, you're literally speaking approximately funding made using an enterprise toward growing their most critical aid; human useful resource. And the sellers entrusted with gratifying this are you.

Instructional design learner and context evaluation

For a given academic aim and context, we need to describe strategies and sources for acquiring statistics about the target population, performance setting, and gaining knowledge of the setting. Analyze and describe the general traits of a goal population and analyze and describe the contextual traits of the eventual overall performance and instructional settings. assess want to identify goal(s) behavior instructional evaluation analyze learners and Contexts Write overall performance objectives Revise guidance develop evaluation gadgets increase academic strategy broaden And pick educational substances layout and conduct Formative evaluation layout and conduct Summative evaluation. "The hazard is now not analyzing the traits of a target audience is assuming that every one newbie are alike. A fair extra not unusual error is assuming that the learners are like the designers. "The maximum important element for a dressmaker to remember about the target market is particular earlier gaining knowledge of".

If we needed to reduce all of instructional psychology to simply one precept, all of us might also finish that the maximum critical single factor influencing studying is what the learner already knows. Verify this and teach him/her for that reason. Although there are a few disagreements among specialists on this vicinity, all might agree that I.Q. is not a degree of a few worldwide, qualitative element which includes 'good brains'. On thinking about gender, ethnicity, and racial group traits, we need to keep in mind those variations now not due to the fact contributors of one gender or racial organization manner information differently, but because contributors of gender, ethnic, or racial institution tend to have not unusual stories because of their group members that may be quite distinctive from the ones had using individuals of different agencies. In different words, even as it's far critical to recall those variations, make sure now not to fall into the trap of stereotyping.

Learner analysis

Now not most effective should the clothier decide what's to be trained, but also the characteristics of the rookies, the contexts in which the coaching might be added, and the contexts wherein the ability will sooner or later be used. Learner analysis; who are they and what are their traits? Target populace and try-out freshmen? We can refer to those newbies because of the goal populace. Target populace is a summary representation of the widest possible variety of users and strive-out learners are the ones newbies who're to be had to the clothier at the same time as the training is being evolved. It's far assumed that these try-out rookies are contributors to the target populace. The intention of learner analysis finds out lots of facts about your newcomers as viable. The statistics collected from the analysis can help decide what academic content is needed and in which the preparation should start. Of direction, some novices will recognize greater than others and each person does now not examine the equal way. But, the learner evaluation can help you discover the learner traits that want to be considered while you layout your training. What records do designers need to recognize approximately their target population? Beneficial statistics include entry behaviors, previous know-how of the topic place, Attitudes closer to content material and capability transport gadget, educational motivation, academic, and capability tiers, widespread learning options, Attitudes towards the corporation giving the preparation, and organization characteristics.

 Four important regions of traits are 1. Cognitive – intellectual/intellectual competencies 2. Physiological – physical abilities 3. Affective – attitudinal issues 4. Social – specifically crucial for group work 4 categories of Learner traits (from Smith & Ragan) Similarities [among novices] differences [among inexperienced persons] stable [through the years] changing [over the years]. Sensory Capacities, information Processing, types and situations of gaining knowledge of, IQ, Cognitive patterns, Psychosocial traits, Gender, ethnicity, and racial organization.

Improvement tactics –highbrow –Language –Psychosocial –ethical: improvement kingdom. Prior learning – fashionable –specific gaining knowledge of style every other learner function to don't forget is studying style. Although you can now not be capable of creating coaching to suit every form of gaining knowledge of fashion, understanding the getting to know fashion can help to offer options. The following is a list of common kinds of learning patterns: 1. Tactile/Kinesthetic college students analyze exceptional whilst bodily engaged in a "hands-on" hobby. They do now not need to simply study about something, they want to do it. Gaining knowledge of fashion: 2. visual/Perceptual; students study fine by searching. Demonstrations from the blackboard, diagrams, graphs, and charts are all treasured gear for them. visual learners do not forget high-quality what they see-photographs, diagrams, flow charts, timelines, movies, and demonstrations. Studying style: 3. auditory newbies prefer facts presented in an oral language layout. In a schoolroom placing, they advantage from being attentive to lectures and collaborating in group discussions. 4. active as opposed to Reflective energetic: newcomers tend to retain and recognize information first-class through doing something active with it (discussing or applying it or explaining it to others) Reflective: newbies prefer to consider it quietly first. "Let's suppose it via first" is the reflective learner's reaction. Studying style: 5. Sequential as opposed to international Sequential: learners choose to continue step-with the aid of step, in an orderly manner, to the stop result. They anticipate studying something they are shown right away. Worldwide: novices decide upon an overview or "huge image" of what they may be going to do first before studying a complicated technique. They like having a map or an instance so that they are where they're headed and what they are running toward.

Getting to know fashion on gathering the facts includes interviews or questionnaires/surveys with those who work with the target population and with individuals of the target populace. Observations of the target populace, published records about age institution: more accepted, however nevertheless be beneficial, and facts/documents created through beginners inside the goal populace.

Implications of Learner; characteristics for design include the pace of the lesson, number of exercise activities, Making the case for relevancy, techniques for gaining and focusing attention, Context of examples and practice activities, amount of shape and employer, kind of remarks to provide, level of learner manage, reading/vocabulary level, quantity and sorts of reinforcement, and the amount of time allowed for guidance, amount and sort of gaining knowledge of steering.

Level of concreteness/abstraction analyzing contexts; context evaluation of overall performance putting

To realize the environment wherein our newcomers may be the use of their new capabilities:

•To decorate the beginners' motivation, feel of educational relevance, and transfer of recent understanding and abilities to the work placing what records do designers need to know approximately the performance setting? Useful records include Managerial or supervisor guide, bodily elements of the site, Social elements of the website, and Relevance of skills to the administrative center. a way to gather the facts; Observations – offer important data no longer most effective for direct input to the assignment however additionally for enhancing the competencies and information of designers.

•On-website traveling – to gather records from ability newbies and executives and to study the work environment wherein the brand new skill will be used.

Interview Output: 1. an outline of the bodily and organizational surroundings where the skills might be used. 2. A list of any unique elements which could facilitate or interfere with the learners' use of the brand new competencies. Performance placing Context evaluation of getting to know environment determining what's and what need to be. What's: an assessment of the placing in which instruction will take vicinity? What must be: facilities, gadgets, and resources that accurately guide the intended training what information do designers want to realize about the learning surroundings? Useful records include Compatibility of the website with the educational requirement, adaptability of the site to simulate place of business, adaptability for transport approaches, and gaining knowledge of site constraints affecting design and delivery.

The way to acquire the information: The process to comply within reading the studying context is to agenda visit to one or extra schooling sites, to schedule interviews with teachers, managers of the sites, and inexperienced persons. Take a look at the website online in use and imagine its use for your coaching Output 1.an outline of the quantity to which the site can be used to supply schooling on skills with a purpose to be required for transfer to the place of work. 2. A list of any boundaries which could have extreme implications for the task. Mastering environment normal analysis guidelines: 1. Make a list of the vital data – and check it off as soon as you have it. 2. Increase a strategy for coming across the information you want. 3. Broaden a method for making feel of the records. 4. Cultivate relationships with various those who might be in a position to inform your evaluation - instructor/boss - determine/accomplice -

peers/colleagues - one of the pleasant resources: the novices!

• Learner evaluation – The more you understand approximately your rookies, but the higher your practice might be – Don't expect that all inexperienced persons are identical – View range of newcomers as energy.

• Context analysis – recognize the real putting where a learner, in the long run, will perform the capabilities – training normally takes vicinity in a specific putting, so search for methods to help rookies transfer their studying.

Chapter Four

Seasonal Affective Disorder

The seasonal affective ailment is a mental mood sickness this is characterized via lethargy and despair based upon the seasons of the earth. There are two distinct subtypes of the disorder. They're winter seasonal affective disease and summer seasonal affective ailment. Winter sad is extra common and it happens within the months of wintry weather and it spontaneously disappears within the springtime. Summertime unhappiness is just the alternative; depression happens within the spring and the signs and symptoms recede in the wintry weather. Subsyndromal sad is just like seasonal affective sickness but has milder signs and does now not disturb someone's capacity to feature. This paper will awareness specifically on wintry weather seasonal affective disorder. The Diagnostic and Statistical Manual of mental disorders lists unhappy as "a specifier of either bipolar or recurrent predominant depressive episodes."

Epidemiology

This sickness simplest influences a small number of people every year. The seasonal affective disease is anticipated to handiest be recognized in five percent of the populace. Geographical location does play a critical factor in the incidence of the ailment. The ailment is more commonplace amongst people who enjoy an extended iciness and fewer hours of sunlight than humans towards the equator. Even as human beings in all regions of the USA can be identified with seasonal affective disorder, it ordinarily impacts human beings that live north forty tiers in latitude. Apparently, human beings native to Alaska are less possibly to be recognized than people that relocate to that region. Sad is four instances extra commonplace amongst girls than males. This may be because of variations in each sex in biochemical responses to climatic adjustments. In a have a look at Budget, Gati, and Soubiran, adult males tailored to climate changes by lowering their metabolism. Ladies, however, confirmed variable metabolic reactions to temperature increases. This will imply that adult males are extra effective at responding to climatic variables than women due to an organic distinction.

Seasonal affective ailment normally develops around the age of twenty to thirty years vintage and also suggests evidence of big familial predisposition to growing the sickness. Fifty to sixty percent of sufferers with unhappiness have first diploma household which has a chief effective infection. This demonstrates a critical genetic role in the sickness that can also be a predictor for a higher hazard of unhappiness.

After following up with sufferers with sadness five to eleven years after diagnosis, thirty-eight to forty-two percent of sufferers routinely enjoy the signs and symptoms of unhappiness. This indicates that patients with the ailment may be dealt with successfully without relapsing with the same signs.

Symptoms

The symptoms of the seasonal affective disorder are present for the duration of the wintry weather and are not skilled within the spring and summer seasons. frequent signs of sad are "Social withdrawal; reduced interest; sadness; tension", pretty frequent symptoms are "carbohydrate craving; reduced libido; bad excellent of sleep; multiplied sleep; irritability; increased weight; increased appetite" fairly infrequent signs and symptoms are "Suicidal mind; decreased sleep; decreased urge for food." these strange depression signs and symptoms can be lifestyles altering and have to be treated.

Pathology

It is believed that seasonal affective disease is brought about by reduced exposure to sunlight. Its underlying cause is not clean but there are many theories as to what reasons sad. Melatonin is a hormone this is crucial in circadian rhythms and the sleep-wake cycle. Seasonal affective sickness became originally believed to be a peculiar melatonin metabolism, however patients with sad did no longer have any abnormalities of their ranges of melatonin secretion. But, it's far cautioned that sufferers with sadness have extraordinary insensitiveness to mild and can have mild prompted suppression of melatonin in the course of the night. It has been found that vivid light can inhibit nocturnal melatonin secretion of the pineal gland. The research on melatonin and seasonal affective disorder advise melatonin can also play a small component in the disease but it isn't always believed to be the primary reason.

Another idea is that the biological clock is disrupted for the duration of the wintry weather months. The circadian rhythms of sufferers with unhappiness appear to be greater abnormal than wholesome individuals. Their styles in the circadian rhythms deviate from regular and do no longer show the same instances of height as humans without the disease. There is proof that the circadian rhythm disturbances "are worsened by using shorter duration of daylight hours, publicity to cold climate, and growing older." The differences in circadian rhythms of sufferers with sadness may be explained by way of the shorter daylight hours experienced in the wintry weather months.

Even small modifications within the sleep-wake cycle may have large consequences on mood. The mood is prompted through the circadian rhythm and the hours spent wide awake. Strange sleep styles are stated by way of many people with the seasonal affective ailment. Even as unhappy sufferers have a normal homeostatic regulation of sleep, modifications in the sleep-associated occasion are experienced. The sleep-associated activities may be frame temperature, extended rapid eye motion, and much less efficient sleep. This statistics displays how small modifications in sleep can greatly affect a person's mood and can be the motive of sadness.

It is a concept that mild all through one-of-a-kind times of the day may be a cause of seasonal affective sickness. Assessments that determined mild therapy for the duration of various times of the day were completed. The outcomes of observation showed morning light management to be powerful in assuaging signs of seasonal affective disease. Times and duration of daylight are altered relying on the seasons of the year. Special stages of mild for the duration of the day in exceptional seasons may additionally explain why sufferers experience depressive signs and symptoms at some point of sure parts of the months.

Whilst this examination could explain the seasonal affective disease, different studies have no longer had equal consequences. For that reason, we cannot claim that these changes in light times motive seasonal affective ailment. It is argued that humans with unhappiness do no longer all have the identical want for mild at the same times of the day; their circadian rhythms can be advanced or delayed. As an example, a few sufferers may also need extra mild in the morning, and others need more mild inside the nighttime. This makes it tough to determine whether those mild stages for the duration of the day are the cause of seasonal affective disease.

Reduced serotonin features within the brain can be every other reason behind seasonal affective sickness. Sufferers with sad or recurrent main melancholy display depressive symptoms when the mind's serotonin function is lowered by depletions of tryptophan from the weight loss plan, in contrast to normal individuals. Some other look at that regulated hormonal responses with a serotonin-liberating agent mentioned that sufferers with sad had diminished prolactin and cortisol changes. There may be additional evidence that abnormalities inside the serotonin transporter are greater commonplace in human beings with unhappiness than people without the ailment. Sufferers with unhappiness show exceptional serotonin patterns than everyday people. This abnormality can be the reason for seasonal affective disease

That is supported with the aid of a take a look at that "said that consumption of carbohydrates improved the plasma content of tryptophan, as well as serotonin synthesis within the rat mind. This locating is important in discovering the purpose of seasonal affective disease in addition to a powerful remedy. Carbohydrate consumption will increase in sufferers at the same time as they're experiencing the symptoms of unhappiness. This will be explained with the aid of lower serotonin stages; sufferers devour excessive carbohydrates to make amends for this lower.

More guide for this theory is proven by the usage of precise serotonin reuptake inhibitors. Those medications are powerful inside the treatment of seasonal affective ailment at the same time as different medications for despair aren't. They work with the aid of blocking off serotonin from being reabsorbed, consequently growing the quantity of serotonin being used. This leads humans to consider that serotonin is an issue of the sickness as nicely.

Every other exciting concept is that seasonal affective disorder can also relate to rod shortening due to deficient photostatic adjustment, leading to decreased absorption of quanta of light, main to insufficient mild strength believed to be essential for preserving a normal mood. This means that a decreased photoperiod of daylight within the wintry weather does no longer provide people with the shorter rods sufficient time crucial to cultivate a healthful mood. Nonetheless, this principle has no longer been demonstrated to be the underlying cause of seasonal affective sickness.

Mind activity of sad patients varies from healthful individuals. Positron emission tomography or pet scans of sufferers with sadness show a decreased metabolism inside the brain than healthful people. The sufferers with sadness had a greater metabolic hobby on the left facet of their brain within the medial prefrontal cortex. On puppy scans of everyday individuals, there's reduced blood float after shiny-light remedy. Sufferers with sadness showed an increase in the blood goes with flow following this remedy. This is not handiest crucial in determining the cause of the disease; it is also relevant to treatment efficacy. Patients with unhappy reply well to vivid-mild remedy. Specific mind hobby is located in these patients and needs to be further explored to decide the underlying purpose. Although the actual purpose isn't always recognized, all of those natural changes elude an imbalance of organic elements.

Treatment

The maximum common treatment for the seasonal affective disease is phototherapy. Phototherapy or light remedy "involved exposure to visible mild generating at lead 2500 lx at eye stage". In line with Merriam Webster dictionary, Lux or lx is "a unit of illumination identical to the direct illumination on a surface that is anywhere one meter from a uniform point source of one candle depth or equal to one lumen according to square meter" (Merriam Webster). This mild need to be obtained by using unique lights because lighting with the house is typically around a hundred lx. According to Timby & Smith, "The frequency and length for phototherapy can range, however, a commonplace prescription is for the patient to take a seat with the aid of the mild supply from half-hour to two hours consistent with day, ideally inside the early morning hours". Additionally, direct eye touch with the light isn't always required. A convenient shape of treatment is a phototherapy mild inside the bedroom that is set to an automatic timer. They remove darkness from at a predawn schedule. The mild passes via the eyes and is thought to cause a decline in melatonin, which may additionally alleviate seasonal affective sickness signs and symptoms.

In line with Partonen & Lonnqvist, phototherapy for two hours within the morning for seven consecutive days "led to enhancements of sixty-seven percent of patients with mild depressive episodes and 40% of those with mild to severe depressive episodes" (1998). The treatment has a surprisingly short onset and simplest takes approximately four days to start looking at signs of remission. This remedy does now not cure the affected person of seasonal affective disorder. Signs will go back if the remedy is ceased. This remedy is likewise powerful for children and children.

In recognition of the type of light, complete spectrum mild isn't always required for seasonal affective sickness treatment. White and green mild are superior for a remedy to pink mild. Additionally, ultraviolet or UV mild is not required for treatment. In truth, ultraviolet mild is extra powerful in treating abnormal symptoms along with those visible with unhappiness.

Even as this remedy seems most fulfilling, some accept it as true that the fantastic effects are simplest seen due to the placebo impact. Others propose that the placebo effect was now not the cause for fulfillment. Rosenthal states "that a placebo explanation of the therapeutic impact of light might not be achievable, given that a placebo tended to bring about a more speedy and variable time course of reaction and relapse, a slow decline in treatment efficacy with time, and a variable difference between remedy effect of brilliant and dim mild." This remedy can also be effective due to the fact the light is a conditioned stimulus that creates euthymic states as a response. Sufferers may additionally consider that they're experiencing depressive signs and symptoms as a result of loss of light. Their temper can be accelerated because of the conditioned stimulus of the light. This is notion to be wrong due to the fact the effects of mild remedies final longer than hypnosis.

Although this treatment appears best, there are negative aspects effects. Eye pressure and headache are common lawsuits of sufferers prescribed with light remedies. Medicinal drugs also are used as a treatment for seasonal affective ailment. These treatments are typically used if the light remedy does now not work. Antidepressants are effective at treating sad. Selective serotonin reuptake inhibitors are taken into consideration powerful at the same time as different antidepressants are not. Easy lifestyle modifications can be an easy way to mitigate the depressive signs accomplice with the seasonal affective disease. Those life changes are:

• "Take walks outdoor, ideally around noon. Try to move out of doors for an hour a day.

• Avoid using sun shades or contact lenses that might be covered to shield UV radiation due to the fact this interferes with mild transmission to the pineal gland.

• Add greater lamps and brighter lighting fixtures at domestic and work.

• Trim shrubs and bushes from around windows to allow in milder.

• Use translucent curtains or sunglasses as opposed to

heavy drapes.
• Sleep and work in east-going through rooms"
Those easy lifestyle changes could be a powerful remedy for the ones experiencing milder symptoms and can reduce signs of sadness.

The seasonal affective disease is a mental sickness wherein melancholy takes place all through an equal time every twelve months. Normally sufferers experience signs and symptoms in the iciness months, however, other time cycles are viable. It best affects a small wide variety of human beings however its odd despair signs may be existence changing. The direct purpose of the disease is unknown however is idea to be because of variations in the quantity of light each day. Light therapy is an efficacious remedy for the seasonal affective disease. Other treatments include antidepressant medicinal drugs and lifestyle modifications. This record is crucial in studying the way to perceive the ailment and ways to deal with sufferers.

Seasonal affective disorder (unhappy) became first described as a syndrome related to depressive episodes that recur and remit annually in sure seasons. The diagnostic and statistical guide of mental issues includes a seasonal pattern specifier that may be implemented to recurrent essential depressive disease or bipolar I or II ailment in cases where the principal depressive episodes recur in a particular season and fully remit or trade to mania or hypomania at a feature time of year.
An envisioned ten to twenty percent of recurrent despair

cases comply with a seasonal sample. Even though a summer sample of recurrence is viable, the most important pattern involves fall/iciness despair with spring/summer remission. In U.S. network surveys, sad incidence degrees from 9.7 percent in New Hampshire to 1.4 percent in Florida. In North the US, unhappy occurrence increases with range, however, the correlation is non-sizable in other parts of the sector.

It is vital to introduce the idea of seasonality and outline it right here. The assembling of seasonality is quite typically allotted inside the popular populace, and the syndrome of sadness appears to symbolize an excessive alongside the seasonality continuum. Young adults and women are most in all likelihood to enjoy unhappy with the suggested gender distinction starting from 2:1 to 9. Sad additionally has been diagnosed in children and kids. They are no longer constrained to mood disorders, seasonal styles were recognized in bulimia nervosa, tension issues, and different psychiatric situations.

Theories

Pathogenic theories for unhappiness have centered on neurotransmitters, hormones, circadian rhythm dysregulation, genetic polymorphisms, and psychological elements. In human beings, the rate of serotonin turnover in the brain is lowest inside the winter season, and the rate of serotonin production will increase with luminosity. Monoaminergic task and depletion studies implicate serotonergic structures in the pathogenesis of sad. People with sadness effectively dealt with brilliant light remedy relapse whilst serotonin and catecholamine ranges are depleted. Efficacy of the serotonin reuptake inhibitors (SSRIs) in unhappy treatment provides indirect evidence for the role of serotonin in sad. Taken cumulatively, research shows that serotonin and catecholamines might also play a role in both the pathophysiology of unhappiness and the antidepressant impact of light therapy.

The phase-shift speculation proposes that the frame's sleep-wake cycle is segment-delayed in sad with appreciate to the environmental mild-dark cycle, and is primarily based on observations of not on time onset of sleep, melatonin, frame temperature, and cortisol rhythms in some unhappy patients. Wintry weather worsening of temper become associated with indirect measures of phase-delay in an Australian community pattern. Mild therapy administered in the morning can segment-improve circadian rhythms in individuals with sad who are segment-not on time. The magnitude of the antidepressant reaction to morning light remedy has been associated with the degree of phase-develop accomplished. But, it remains doubtful how a phase delay can also result in melancholy.

The photon-count hypothesis shows those shorter photoperiods (hours of daylight hours) and/or less excessive mild within the wintry weather effects in an insufficient dose of mild (i.e., fewer photons) to the retina in unhappy-inclined individuals. A prospective, longitudinal take a look found a wonderful correlation among melancholy severity and photoperiod and two measures of light depth (mins of sunshine and global radiation) in unhappy sufferers. A current mild therapy meta-evaluation discovered a dose-reaction courting among light remedy depth and diploma of development within the traditional, however no longer within the ordinary, depressive symptoms.

Individuals with unhappiness might also reply to longer nights in wintry weather with an extended length of nocturnal melatonin launch, a hormone that can sell sleep. Whilst measuring lively melatonin secretion below steady dim mild, Wehr, et al., discovered that people with unhappiness had an extended length of melatonin launch at some point of wintry weather than summertime whereas controls did not. That is analogous to the lengthened duration of melatonin release in some mammals that indicators seasonal adjustments in reproductive activity. It is feasible that the handiest human beings with sadness have retained the potential to track seasons in this way, which might explain the seasonal presentation of unhappiness.

Research of twins, families with a sad proband, and other extraordinarily homogeneous organizations indicate that sad maybe, in element, an inherited disease. Candidate genes associated with serotonin and dopamine and molecular components of the circadian clock had been investigated.

Polymorphisms within the serotonin transporter promoter area (five-HTTLPR) and in the serotonin 2A receptor (five-HT2A-1483G/A) had been related to sad in a few studies but now not others. The dopamine-four receptor gene (DRD4) seven-repeat allele changed into related to binge eating behavior in a sample of girls with unhappiness. Neuronal PAS area protein 2 (NPAS2), a transcription issue expressed inside the circadian clock, turned into implicated in diurnal version (preference for morning or night) in a sad case-manage look at. Those effects endorse that unhappy and particular unhappy symptom may be regulated by way of different genetic factors, each contributing a small-to-slight quantity of risk. Current etiological models have attempted to combine organic and mental mechanisms in explaining sad onset and preservation. The younger twin vulnerability model proposes separate vulnerabilities amongst individuals with a history of unhappiness: a physiological vulnerability to revel in odd symptoms at some stage in the winter and a pair of) a psychological vulnerability to broaden cognitive and affective signs and symptoms of depression in reaction to the vegetative symptoms. young devised this hypothesis based on his finding that people with unhappiness retrospectively acknowledged the onset of fatigue, hypersomnia, and accelerated urge for food previous to growing cognitive and effective signs and symptoms. One-of-a-kind pathophysiological mechanisms may additionally account for the distinctive vulnerabilities proposed, leading to the heterogeneity of findings from studies addressing the etiology and treatment of sad.

Evidence is developing that cognitive and behavioral models of despair may additionally observe as unhappy. In go-sectional studies, people with unhappy and non-seasonal melancholy suggested, in addition, bad attributional patterns and comparable bad computerized thoughts and dysfunctional attitudes. A prospective, longitudinal have a look observed that girls with a sad record encouraged greater common poor computerized thoughts than non-depressed controls throughout all seasons, with peak terrible automatic concept frequency within the wintry weather. Two research discovered that ruminative coping (i.e., focusing on the causes and outcomes of depressed temper), as assessed inside the fall, anticipated the severity of sad signs all through the following iciness. Behavioral disengagement is underscored using the progression of decline in unhappiness from the reduced capability for amusement in fall to reduced frequency of response-contingent tremendous reinforcement in the wintry weather.

Remedy procedures

The maximum extensively used and drastically investigated treatment for sad is the light remedy (i.e., each day exposure to a field containing fluorescent lamps at some point of the symptomatic months). Positive activities, inclusive of studying, aren't prohibited so long as the person can maintain an appropriate position and distance from the unit. concerning the greatest dose, 10,000-lux of the complete spectrum or cool white fluorescent lighting set behind an ultraviolet defend is usual. The endorsed daily length varies from half-hour to two hours per day, and two to four weeks is normally ok to determine responsiveness.

The best controversy surrounds the top-rated timing of light remedies. Head-to-head comparisons recommend that morning light may be greater efficacious than evening mild, but one meta-evaluation determined the biggest mean effect length for morning-plus-nighttime mild. A growing type of transportable, head-established mild visors, smaller desk lamp devices, sunrise simulators, and mild furniture with light-emitting diodes (LEDs) have also been evolved. Greater studies are needed to determine whether those devices are as effective as trendy mild boxes for unhappy.

Tips suggest administering light remedies under the supervision of a qualified professional. In clinical settings, the unique light therapy prescription is regularly tailored to the individual's sleep-wake styles, aspect results, and alternatives. Facet effects to mild remedy are usually mild and ameliorated via dose manipulations, but can consist of headache, eyestrain, and psychomotor agitation. Relative contraindications for mild remedies encompass certain retinal sicknesses, medicinal drugs that grow retinal sensitivity to mild, and a history of mania or hypomania.

A pooled evaluation of light remedy research concluded that 53.3% of people with unhappiness met standards for complete remission with light remedy. However, only 43% of individuals with mild to extreme unhappy signs and symptoms remitted with light therapy. Supplementary and alternative remedies have been evolved due to the fact mild remedy isn't enough for all unhappy patients.

Clinically, SSRIs and other psychotropic medications are often used as an accessory or alternative to mild remedies. An initial study discovered that light remedy plus tablet placebo (50%) had a better remission price than fluoxetine plus dim mild placebo (25%). maximum currently, a five-center Canadian look at observed similar remission rates for mild therapy plus pill placebo (fifty four%) and fluoxetine plus dim light placebo (50%). In a retrospective analysis of unhappy outpatients in Finland, seventy-three percent of eight sufferers handled with moclobemide and 61% of eleven sufferers treated with fluoxetine replied over six weeks. A look at that randomized eight women with unhappy to blended light remedy and citalopram or mild therapy and tablet placebo discovered no difference in the conditions at put up-remedy, but more efficacy for aggregate treatment thirty-four weeks later. A randomized trial comparing sertraline to tablet placebo for eight weeks tested more upgrades with sertraline on measures of despair severity.

Similar to antidepressants, other pharmacologic retailers display promise in treating unhappiness. One open-label study located that modafinil, a novel wake-selling agent, confirmed a 67% reaction fee, defined as a 50% or greater reduction in sad symptoms, indicating that randomized, managed research can be warranted. Propranolol, administered in the morning in open treatment for two weeks, produced a 73% reaction charge in a pattern of thirty-three, unhappy patients, even though not all remedy profits were maintained over the following weeks inside the lively drug continuation organization as opposed to placebo. Fifty destiny research should observe propranolol's melatonin-suppressing effects as a mediator of antidepressant response in unhappy.

Our group has currently advanced and pilot-examined a sad-tailored version of cognitive-behavioral therapy (CBT), modeled upon Beck's cognitive remedy, fifty-one that is an empirically confirmed treatment for non-seasonal depression. The CBT for unhappy protocol includes 90-minute periods two times per week over six weeks (general of twelve periods) brought in institution layout. The behavioral component uses satisfactory pastime scheduling to counteract "hibernation" by way of developing wintertime pursuits. Negative cognitions are diagnosed and challenged, along with the mind related to wintry weather, light availability, seasonal environmental cues, and climate. Relapse-prevention emphasizes the usage of CBT abilities in the course of next fall/wintry weather seasons in response to anticipatory poor thoughts approximately winter or unhappy-related conduct adjustments.

Our feasibility look at located that CBT, mild therapy, and their mixture had been similarly powerful in the extreme remedy of sad. At a naturalistic one-year comply with-up, individuals dealt with CBT, without or with adjunct mild remedy, evidenced much less severe despair on patient- and interviewer-rated measures. No CBT-treated player met standards for a full sad episode recurrence relative to 62.5% of contributors dealt with mild therapy alone. We have completed a bigger sample, multiyear trial comparing CBT, mild remedy, and aggregate therapy to wait-listing management with manuscript guidance underway.

Aerobic workout interventions, that have confirmed efficacy in the remedy of non-seasonal predominant despair, are being explored in sad. Pinchas, et al., compared mild therapy to cardio workout (i.e., each day classes on a stationary bicycle separated through five minutes of rest, every concerning a five-minute heat up accompanied with the aid of ten minutes of simple pedaling and ten minutes of pedaling at seventy five-percent maximal heart fee), with both remedies administered for one week in the course of the afternoon, in a small sample of ladies with unhappy. Exercise and light therapy had been related to similar and big reductions in despair severity and an improved price of oxygen intake relative to an untreated control group, suggesting that normalization of everyday power expenditure might also underlie the efficacy of both treatments.

Even though morning exercise might be useful inside the remedy of unhappiness, based totally on the idea that it might result in a section-advance, those consequences advise that the timing of exercising might not be important to the antidepressant outcomes of exercising on sad. However, exercising past due at night might be contraindicated in unhappiness because it could lead to a segment-postpone within the onset of melatonin release the subsequent night in human beings.

In healthful controls, aerobic exercise has done below brilliant (2,500- to 4,000-lux) lighting fixtures appears to be greater useful than both workout under common indoor lights and no workout for extraordinary signs and symptoms and energy. Consequently, outdoor workouts or combining aerobic exercise with mild therapy would possibly have software for sad but has now not yet been examined. Larger controlled trials are needed to in addition take a look at exercising as an alternative or adjunctive treatment approach in unhappy.

Chapter Five

Schizophrenia and Learning Outcomes

Schizophrenia is a mental ailment or contamination that impacts a lot of two million individuals every year. It is an intellectual ailment that cannot be cured and can have extreme and even disabling signs and symptoms which can have an effect on people their whole lives. Many people estimate that as many as one percentages of the sector populace are laid low with schizophrenia. Many consider that the disease can affect ladies and men equally; however, most would agree that men are regularly affected at earlier a while and often greater severely than women. A few others assume that the numbers of people affected by Schizophrenia are towards nearly one in every one hundred people, as does Professor John McGrath of Queensland Centre for mental health studies. there is a strong consider using some that schizophrenia does occur extra frequently in males than it does in females and that during exclusive areas of the world the numbers of cases of schizophrenia range. The simplest aspect that the professional seem to agree on is that that is no clear motive for this disorder.

Symptoms
As it is actually with maximum intellectual ailments or

problems, symptoms do now not continually fit precisely and may truly constitute a selection of ailments and problems; so it is very important to rule out all feasible bodily issues and ailments before thinking about schizophrenia as a diagnosis. Also, it's well worth noting that many mental ailments and issues proportion not unusual signs, and schizophrenia isn't any extraordinary in this recognition. There are several symptoms associated with Schizophrenia.

Distorted perceptions of reality: because schizophrenics live a life that includes delusions and hallucinations, they frequently have a much-skewed view of truth. They regularly find themselves residing of their personal global or fact. Hallucinations and Illusions: Hallucinations and illusions are very commonplace for humans laid low with schizophrenia. Hallucinations can arise by the use of any sense belief, but auditory (hearing voices) is the most commonplace form of hallucination for schizophrenics. Those voices can communicate to the schizophrenic, recommend them, carry on normal conversations with them, and direct them to do sure things. An illusion is an actual sensory stimulus, but one that the schizophrenic individual interrupts wrongly.

Delusions: A fable is considered a false notion that has no rational basis. A person with schizophrenia may also have feelings of being persecuted or spied upon. Disordered thinking: The schizophrenic is often not able to assume absolutely or "think straight". Emotional Expression: the ones tormented by schizophrenia regularly display little to no emotion or even go as some distance as changing their speech patterns to expression stuffed speech to a monotone flat speech. Normal as opposed to strange tiers-even though each person that is taken into consideration regularly can also exhibit a number of the symptoms indexed above a number of the time; schizophrenics reveal at least two or greater of the symptoms in a greater chronic or persistent way.

Types of Schizophrenia

There special types of sub-categories of schizophrenia and all of the sub-categories of schizophrenia are defined and diagnosed via their predominant characteristic or signs and symptoms.

* Paranoid Schizophrenia. The main signs which are exhibited on this sub-category are feeling of persecution or conspiracy and auditory hallucinations.

* Disorganized Subtype. This sub-category is characterized by intense incapacity to prepare and arrange everyday living sports inclusive of bathing, dressing, and eating. Hallucinations and delusions are generally much less visible in this sub-class.

* Catatonic Subtype. This sub-category is one of the most excessive degrees of schizophrenia. An instance of the sub-class might be someone lying in the fetal position and able to reply to any stimulus. This state of schizophrenia can also include repetitive and meaningless sounds and moves although. In other words, the man or woman can be void of any actual verbal exchange but make mimicking sounds or actions mocking those human beings around.

* Undifferentiated subtype. This subclass is used for people with a diagnosis of schizophrenia, but that doesn't suit absolutely one of the different sub-categories. It's far a form of "trap all" sub-category.

* Residual subtype. This sub-category refers to individuals

with a schizophrenic diagnosis, but that isn't currently exhibiting any of the intense signs associated with the infection. Those could be individuals on medicinal drugs or humans with a duration of a type of remission or absence of the greater extreme symptoms.

Remedy

As with most mental ailments and issues, schizophrenics gain from a ramification of remedies and medications. There seem to be two principal troubles to first cope with while being concerned for a person with schizophrenia and people are; make sure the person is taking their remedy regularly and try to offer a secure and relaxed domestic environment. Those are just the beginning steps and there are extra precise remedies that are available.

In all cases of schizophrenia, antipsychotic medicinal drugs are almost continually utilized. a number of the older medicines were available because of the 1950s. These tablets; Thorazine, Haldol, Prolixin, Navane, and others had been known as "neuroleptics" because they brought about neurological side consequences and had little impact on the emotional expressiveness of the sufferers. Because in 1989 a brand new series of medicinal drugs were added such as; Clozaril, Risperdal, Zyprexa, Abilify, and a few others. that medicinal drug normally takes two to four weeks to truly take effect and feature fewer side consequences neurologically, but they all do nonetheless have a few and sundry side results. it can take time to adjust the medication to attain the precise dosage for every character. One essential drawback to these new medicines is that failure to use them or abnormal use can reason the schizophrenic person to relapse extra fast. Nevertheless, with all of the aspect results and problems, antipsychotic medicinal drugs are required for maximum schizophrenic patients.

Schizophrenics regularly have troubles with daily dwelling talents, relationships, conversation capabilities, and motivation. For these reasons, it's far almost vital that schizophrenics get some kind of psychosocial assistance. Periods with psychologists or psychiatrists are very essential to those patients' social growth. That is even extra so essential in view that most people of instances start at the early teen a while when social growth is so crucial. Own family counseling with the patient in a collection setting is also essential. Among medications and the right counseling, most schizophrenics are capable of life close to regular lives.

Teaching individuals with Schizophrenia

Thus far we've got mentioned what humans identified with schizophrenia can do to help themselves, or even what family and family members can do to help, but there's nevertheless the problem of the way to train these people in our lecture rooms. There are numerous proper hints as to how educators can deal with the troubles confronted with teaching students with schizophrenia. The primary and most important problem for the educator positioned on this function is to be nicely educated about the illness. Beware of available treatments, reasons, and symptoms so you can speak intelligently with dad and mom or college students' issues concerning education. Reduce strain inside the room as much as feasible. Work with the scholar with schizophrenia to help them set practical academic and social desires. Set up ordinary conferences with the circle of relatives or pupils to speak about issues, issues, or successes. As a great deal as possible, encourage participation and interplay between the student with the illness and other students.

Lodges and modifications

With many problems, disabilities, and ailments there may be a variety of problems and learning issues associated with the person. Many schizophrenics will have to get to know disabilities about their mental disorders. Addressing motels and adjustments for individuals with schizophrenia is as individual as all people. Numerous lodges can be used to make the schizophrenic's instructional revel in an advantageous one.

Stress appears to be one aspect that could get worse the schizophrenic's possibilities for achievement. Relieving pressure from the surroundings is one factor that has to be used. Permitting the student to have a quiet secluded vicinity to finish assignments and tests is one manner to offer the student a strain loose environment. Internet publications also are a manner for those students to be able to complete courses in a secure and stress unfastened environment. The primary accommodation that may be provided is precedence registration. With precedence registration, college students can pick instances and teachers as a way to satisfactory match into their recurring and match their needs. Those are simply a completely few lodges that can be comfortably available for those college students.

Schizophrenia is an infection that influences many Americans and people globally. It is a contamination that can be disabling if not dealt with appropriately; however, can be only a minor hassle if treated nicely and addressed early. With the variety of instances growing and with the high time for onset of schizophrenia being commonly early young adults and early Nineteen Twenties, college-age students are substantially affected. It becomes critical for educators to end up more aware of the sickness and greater privy to a way to cope with this contamination and the scholars that have it.

Schizophrenia is likewise a disorder that affects about one percent of the sector populace, has a ten percent suicide fee, an envisioned $20 billion in lost productivity, and $11.1 billion in medical prices within the United States in 1980. The number one traits are disturbing language, communication, thought, and perception. There are wonderful forms of signs and symptoms, the nice (atypical activity, inclusive of delusions and hallucinations) and the poor (lack of hobby, consisting of avolition, affective blunting). Davidson (1993, p. 2) additionally identifies three phases of the ailment manner, every of which offers its very own unique problems. Onset starts with social ability deterioration, and problems finishing normal tasks. The extreme section encompasses such gadgets as delusions, hallucinations, and distorted questioning. Eventually, the remission segment is marked using the passing of the distortions, with a return to greater regular functioning, even though in many instances not as effective as before the onset. Relying upon the phase and severity of the disorder, a patient may also have seriously exclusive mental fields as properly. However, inexperienced (1996) factors out that during a literature overview, it's been shown that the degree of psychosis does no longer acts as an indicator of the subsequent restoration.

Schizophrenia may be expressed in a patient via high-quality and/or bad signs. Both superb and negative signs and symptoms typically result in mastering problems, though through exclusive mechanisms. This especially includes (for fine signs and symptoms), derailment, tangentiality, incoherence, illogicality, circumstantiality, strain, distractible speech, and clanging. For negative signs, the results encompass psychomotor poverty, motivation, apathy, loss of vanity, and reduced concern for praise and reinforcements.

The effects of both spectrums are exhibited in studying deficits in unique regions, inclusive of reduced attention, terrible abstract questioning, poor making plans and hassle fixing, negative reminiscence, reduced verbal talents, terrible organizational competencies, choice among relevant and irrelevant stimuli, poor flexible moving of attention, terrible contrast of earlier stimuli to contemporary stimuli, altered evaluative higher methods, impoverished cognitive schema, visual impairments, and chunking impairments.

Schizophrenia also can be defined as an incapacity to sustain an intentional cognizance to attention. This incapability can lead to a lack of control over the mental procedures. The affected person is at instances passive inside their very own mind. Additionally, it appears that the affected person has a lack of ability to "self-edit", ensuing in each verbal and internal established however irrelevant responses. As a result of this inability to direct a train of thought, get the right of entry to long-term memory is compromised.

Effects on cognitive feature

Schizophrenic patients had been studied extensively for cognitive functioning. Even though not all schizophrenic sufferers exhibit cognitive deficits, there may be adequate information to reveal that these defects do arise with regularity.

Popular testing of Schizophrenics suggests that in specific exams, which include the Hiscock pressured-choice technique, schizophrenics with cognitive impairments scored with 84.72% accuracy, in comparison to ninety-seven. Forty-four percent accuracy for those with no cognitive impairment. Moreover, the time on Rey Dot Counting differed appreciably. Cognitively impaired schizophrenics took over 4.6 seconds, even as the ones without impairment have been below three seconds.

Extrapyramidal symptoms (EPS) are a result of lengthy-time period antipsychotic use in schizophrenic patients. Apart from the cognitive deficits resulting from the real disorder technique, it appears that the EPS itself entails the presentation of extra problems in getting to know. While a few non-cognitive elements of EPS which include bradykinesia can alter the consequences while testing for neuropsychological deficits, statistical analysis shows that neuropsychological deficits because of increasing severity of EPS inside the vicinity of mastering aren't related to the bodily manifestations. The decreased capacity on those obligations is the result of deficits in two standard regions, memory and attention. Those are inextricably connected inside the context of studying.

Attention

Interest can be divided into subcategories: preattentive (computerized), and selective (effortful). It has been counseled that the preattentive procedures are impaired, with alternative stimuli inside the environment now not being filtered well. However, it is the selective interest that is extra affected. It appears that schizophrenics have problems with the primary levels of processing new fabric, focusing on the stimuli with selective interest. This will be visible within the act of the affected person's interest is captured using an irrelevant phrase or concept. It is as if the selective interest required to technique the stimuli has been sublimated. This loss of selective attention permits the initial, preattentive styles of attention to proceed and not using controls. Patients describe it as follows: If I am reading, I may additionally suddenly get bogged down at a phrase. It can be any word, even a simple word that I know nicely. Whilst this happens, I'm able to get beyond it. It's as if I'm being hypnotized with the aid of it. It's as though I am seeing the word for the first time and in a special manner from anyone else. It's not a lot that I absorb, it's more like it absorbs me.

It's now not that I will pay attention properly, it's just that I will focus on the foremost problems. I am getting fogged up with all of the specific bits and lose the important matters inside the picture. I locate myself taking note of all forms of tiny things as an alternative to having on with the matters I should be doing.

A principle of this is given by using Knight (1984), who has shown through visible Backward protecting (VBM) exams, that if a significant visual stimulus is offered and immediately followed by a meaningless pattern, the identification of the vast stimuli is decreased in Schizophrenic sufferers. This effect is lessened as the duration of time among considerable stimulus and masking stimulus are offered, however, it in no way reaches the extent of the manipulate institution.

If a hit in bringing the stimuli to the forefront of the cognizance to the procedure, it should be selectively acted on and as compared with previous enjoy. Another time, this potential is impaired. Conversely to quick-term and easy popularity memories, which do now not require energetic attention, searching memory for preceding stories calls for lengthy-term reminiscence which is based totally upon directed interest, that's impaired. That is due to the attention in the schizophrenic being inflexible. The eye can be stuck via another stimulus, in the course of the act of searching long-term reminiscence and it's going to stay there, not transferring returned irrespective of the quantity of interest it definitely holds.

Reminiscence

Reminiscence deficits in Schizophrenia may be severe. One trainer says: He has trouble remembering words. If I ask him to offer me any other word for automobile, he can't. However, if I positioned five phrases down and ask him to discover one which means car, he'll get it. He has little reminiscence for things from one second to the subsequent. He'll study paragraphs and no longer don't forget an element whilst we go to the questions.

This statement itself is indicative of an issue with the retrieval of statistics from memory. There may be additional difficulty with popularity (although no longer as excessive), brief- and lengthy-term reminiscence (with short-term memory storage being greater excessive). Loss of interest span is indicated as the main contributor to this. Students describe their problems with interest:

My thoughts are flying throughout my work and I'm able to appear to assimilate. I can't understand what I've performed. I can't appear to recall what I did the day before this. Someone asks me to consider trouble or something and I find that I'm able to think. I need to go lower back over whatever I research, many, normally. I rely almost completely on what I found out before I was given unwell.

I need help remembering little matters due to the fact I don't pay attention. I'm not paying interest right now. I get distracted pretty smoothly. If there has been a dog barking outdoor, I'd listen to that. I can't stand plenty of noise once I'm working. I come to a phrase like that one there and that I begin gambling around with it.

Medications can positively affect the attention span deficits in schizophrenic patients. By decreasing the stimuli which might be distracting, they allow the affected person to spend the best time on the assignment to hand. But, medications themselves can also affect the reminiscence strategies.

Drowsiness, as experienced with antipsychotic and antiparkinsonian medications, is itself a distractor, with the thoughts wandering extra frequently, making staying on venture extra difficult. The antiparkinsonian pills have moreover been shown to create issues with quick-time period reminiscence.

There are some methods in which the capability to analyze may be affected. Those encompass inner cognitive compensation using the affected person, hospitalizations, medicines, remedies, and educator activities.

Cognitive compensations

Sufferers in an acute stage of Schizophrenia understand the arena as a mass of information, without an overlying view to convey it collectively. They're not able to system sequentially and holistically, as do the majority. As an alternative, they revert to analytical and sequential thinking. This movement in itself shows the symptom of the disease. Human beings without the infection will also revert to this wondering, but most effective in new or unexpected conditions. The truth that the Schizophrenic does so constantly infers that they may be viewing the sector with little regard for stored memories and capacity to peer it as an entire. They have got problem reacting, as they cannot evaluate the action that has been taken with the aid of the stimulus-inducing individual, to a historic perspective of "Does this imply they're mad, unhappy, etc." They must try to pick out upon any available clues to infer the means of their surroundings. With the greater intellectual strain required to attempt to ferret out the reality, the whole from the information comes hyperawareness of the surrounding global via all senses. The affected person sees more acutely, hears tones greater effectively, however nonetheless isn't able to react correctly.

Additionally, the affected person will regularly take control of many capabilities typically processed, autonomically, along with motor control. This splits the attention even similarly, ending with extra confusion, and less motor management. This will bring about some of the bad signs and symptoms of Schizophrenia which includes reduced useful movement. These compensations, even as an essential but unwilled act on part of the patient, aren't useful inside the holistic feel. They are mentally exhausting to the affected person.

Hospitalizations

Hospitalizations, with over fifty percent of the patients requiring two or more hospitalization periods, also affect gaining knowledge. Motivation can be significantly reduced while a person has to interrupt their research and way of life on a common basis. Truly, avoiding hospitalizations as a whole lot as viable permits the patient to hold with as normal a way of life as possible, and will increase shallowness and motivation.

Medicines

Medications used to deal with Schizophrenia can be very efficacious in reducing delusions, hallucinations, and idea disorders, ensuing in a multiplied studying capability. Whilst used judiciously, it has been shown in a few research to be as much as a twenty percent percentile rank boom in various cognitive measures, even though as shown underneath, different studying capabilities are hampered. The antipsychotics, which can be maximum typically used, act to sedate the senses, lowering (filtering) the drift of information this is received. They have got the potential to grow vigilance, but don't have any substantive effect on reminiscence. But, the medications themselves could have side consequences which avoid mastering. These include Drowsiness, blurred imaginative and prescient, and extrapyramidal consequences such as akathisia. Extrapyramidal signs are controlled thru antiparkinsonian pills, which have their own facet results which include blurring and drying of the eyes, and dry mouth. The antiparkinsonian medications have the side impact of decreasing verbal reminiscence, as properly.

Drowsiness affects the potential to pay attention and live on the undertaking, also affecting memory. it can be described as questioning thru molasses. The blurring of the eyes makes it tough for the affected person to read, mainly close to vision. Dry eyes could make the eye put on hard to apply because of consistent itching of the eyes. A dry mouth may interrupt instructions, as a patient may also need to take frequent drinks of fluids. Extrapyramidal signs can reason a difficulty in writing from tremors, inability to live on mission because of restlessness, and disinterest in activities from akinesia.

The effects of drugs on an affected person, as a result, should be carefully evaluated. Doses that can be too high can reason a boom in cognitive functioning troubles as well as other side outcomes. Doses that are too low won't provide sufficient filtration of the stimuli. It is a careful balancing act to limit the overall disruption (unfiltered stimuli + aspect outcomes) to the patient. Best in this way can we attain the most advantageous level of functioning, to be able to range from affected person to patient. Moreover, medicinal drug aspect-effects can also pass with time, being greater excessive with initial dosing, and reducing with the body's acclimation to the medicine through the years.

Cognitive and Psychosocial therapy

Cognitive and Psychosocial treatment options have long

been assumed to haven't any place within the remission of an acute psychotic episode. This becomes the location for medication. According to Beck and Rector (1998), this assumption is untrue. Using cognitive therapy much like that used with depressed sufferers, they consider that mild questioning and empirical testing concerning delusions and hallucinations can help in the abatement of lively psychosis. Once the psychotic episode is in remission, the treatment plans can recognition on the integration of the affected person again into the schoolroom, place of job, and social settings.

It has been hypothesized that sufferers with Schizophrenia can be dealt with further than those with demanding brain harm (TBI). However, this assessment falls upon closer inspection. even as TBI's have an insult and infarction to the brain, it's miles nearly usually to the higher stage processes and the outer layers of the mind, frequently the prefrontal cortex, in those that respond to cognitive rehabilitation. In contrast, it's hypothesized people with Schizophrenia have dysfunctions attributable to mistakes within the brainstem and midbrain structures in addition to the prefrontal cortex.

Seeming to support this view, psychosocial therapy does now not have a strong music document as supported by way of research evidence within the final results of Schizophrenia in keeping with Scott & Dixon (1995). They observe that "on average, person treatment does no longer play an important role in decreasing signs", and the psychodynamic concept failed "to exert any useful results, either on my own or in aggregate with antipsychotic medicinal drugs." They hold to be aware that studies endorse that organization psychotherapy in an institutional putting can also without a doubt be more harmful than useful, at the same time as in an outpatient setting there was no consistent effect on the psychopathology of the disorder. In evaluation, Beck & Rector (1998) accept as true that cognitive remedies can reduce high-quality signs and symptoms, as stated above, as well as bad signs. However, their studies were accomplished with patients who had been actively psychotic, no longer those in remission and trying to go back to normal day-by-day exercises.

Psychosocial competencies education has been proven to have fine influences on the affected person with Schizophrenia when observed at three hundred and sixty-five days, however, those profits have been lost by way of the second one yr. moreover higher complexity obligations had been much less liking to be generalized into the novel situations of existence, as compared to easier obligations including assembly a person's eyes. There has been defined a most desirable putting and technique for producing those effects.

• Engagement of patients, in brief, assailable dialogs to interact with them in personalized goal setting and endorsement of schooling objectives.

• Video demonstrations of the capabilities to be discovered, with Socratic questions and answers to sell vigilance in the video viewing.

• Role-play sporting events wherein the sufferers exercise the one's abilities previously determined inside the video and throughout which plentiful reinforcement, cueing, prompting, and education are supplied.

• Problem-fixing sports wherein the trainer leads the sufferers thru a series of challenges or limitations to the successful implementation of the skills of their natural environments, requiring the sufferers to inductively find out how to triumph over these limitations by using the use of a problem-solving method.

• In vivo homework sports wherein the trainer step by step fades lower back from the sufferers as they use the skills found out earlier in actual-life conditions.

• Preserving the training settings uncluttered and without distracting stimuli.

• Posting photograph charts for clean and easy visible cuing of the mastering goals; capitalizing on dual-channel inputs, each auditory and visual.

• The use of differential remarks, which includes slight social censure or disapproval as well as exuberant advantageous reward, for beside the point and suitable responsiveness to education steps.

• The usage of venture analyses to interrupt down know-how and abilities to be discovered, so that studying can continue incrementally with a shaping paradigm of reinforcing successive approximations.

• Using overlearning and repetition and different generalization-promoting strategies for the switch of getting to know from education to actual-lifestyles settings. There has been an extra type of therapy, supportive psychotherapy, which has all started to expose impact upon the affected person, however remains within the ranges of increase. This remedy consists of objects consisting of strengthening the therapeutic alliance, enacting environmental interventions, placing limits and prohibitions, and undermining maladaptive defenses while strengthening adaptive defenses. It should be cited, that all types of therapy are based totally upon the assumption that the patient has enough cognitive functioning and learning capacity to advantage.

Supporting college students with Schizophrenia

Educators and therapists can help sufferers acquire their highest quality mastering with expertise and assistance in several areas, which include: attendance, attention, imaginative and prescient troubles, comprehension, delusions and hallucinations, sedation, regression, trouble solving, and organization, responsiveness, extrapyramidal signs, and symptoms.

patients with Schizophrenia can also have attendance issues for several motives such as hospitalizations, "drug vacations" (times when a drug is stopped for a time frame, regularly to present relief from aspect-consequences), and frustration with progress. Encouraging sufferers to go back to high school, being compassionate instead of angry, and working with times that aspect-effects of drugs are much less extreme all can inspire the nice attendance viably.

Interest problems with each contamination and medication arise from having to replace duties regularly, or from distractors. Movements, to assist college students to keep most interest, include: maintaining initiatives brief, and uncomplicated, the use of auditory, visible, and stimulus (alternate writing with studying, and many others.), and asking questions concretely to refocus the pupil. Moreover, it's been shown that attention remediation has been helpful in interest span deficits. Options for this encompass schooling in self-training throughout a task and education using PC.

Imaginative and prescient troubles affect the scholars'

ability to stay on the project, as they could either no longer see virtually, or are continuously having to rub their eyes. Patients with blurred imaginative and prescient can see at a distance better than near. Using large print, colored paper (or carrying colored, which include yellow, sunshades), avoidance of fluorescent lights, and magnifying glasses were shown to be of assist. Dry eyes can be assisted through the usage of saline drops.

Comprehension is affected in schizophrenics because of their decreased capability to suppose abstractly, in addition to decreased interest. Retaining the material to be understood short and succinct, after which asking concrete questions can assist within the comprehension and retainment of the material.

Delusions and Hallucinations are very detrimental to mastering because the patient is in a psychological kingdom wherein their reality is altered. There are several ways to assist these sufferers for the duration of their studying manner. Avoidance of emotionally charged conditions can assist save you the triggering of delusions. They're much more likely to analyze authentic data, rather than emotional. Moreover, many sufferers with Schizophrenia have identified strategies that they could use to both "encapsulate" (basically, to place in the heritage) or decrease the severity of the assault. Asking the scholar approximately those strategies ahead, so that the trainer can train them to apply them when wished is useful. Continuing to live with the subject matter, and no longer turn out to be a therapist to the affected person at some stage in those instances, with common cues to refocus the eye is also a success.

Sedation is a commonplace facet-impact of a few of the

medicinal drugs used to treat Schizophrenia. Lodging for the scholar is paramount. Finishing greater complex responsibilities earlier within the day is useful. A bodily pastime can help to offset sedation, even just a quick walk whilst they are feeling mainly fatigued. Taking a short nap, even for a half-hour is beneficial using college students as properly.

Intellectual regression within the form of the lack of abstract questioning capacity also can be visible within the schizophrenic-affected person. The use of much less abstract and more concrete questions is first-rate. The identical give-up result can be completed, although with a greater circuitous route. The affected person will also be affected by deficits with hassle solving and company. Coaching the scholar to actively and consciously hassle solve is critical (including: discover the hassle, creating a plan, following the plan, comparing the outcomes). Writing the trouble and solution out for some of the special eventualities can be beneficial.

A loss of responsiveness to the assignment at hand, or to the environment in trendy is not uncommon in schizophrenic sufferers. That is a hard situation to deal with, as you are not provided with remarks as you continue. Whilst there's no outdoor expression, these sufferers may additionally nevertheless be experiencing internal sensation, and now not be capable of explicit it. Retaining a tremendous attitude and not retreating from the pupil is crucial.

Extrapyramidal signs are physical manifestations that result from the usage of antipsychotics over a long time period. There aren't any specific interventions that can be used apart from selling tolerance. This consists of within the class putting, wherein different freshmen need to be knowledgeable about the bodily manifestations, and within the educator, that the learner will often no longer offer neat work, and written work won't be continually in the given timelines.

Reminiscence impairment, especially implicit as mentioned in advance, can be offset by using "errorless studying". whilst a patient has requested the solution to a query, and they offer the wrong answer and are eventually informed the right solution, they're taking part in "errorful studying" along with while a patient is advised "I am taking into account something clear, cold, and wet" after which are given the chance to reply till they guess successfully or a given time period elapses. Errorless studying is when a learner is told the state of affairs and then the solution along with "I am considering something clean, bloodless, and yet, I'm deliberating Ice."; the learner will remember that solution. In the errorful learning, there are hypotheses: that the patient has trouble figuring out whether a stimulus changed internally or externally generated after a time lag occurs; and all answers being remembered thru implicit memory, with next confusion. With errorless mastering, with the best solution being furnished, the patient has the handiest one stimulus to take into account and is much more likely to don't forget it effectively.

Schizophrenia is a sickness that strikes many human beings at the same time as they may be younger, while they are nonetheless of their getting to know and formative years. As a result, the deficits in interest and memory that result have long-lasting consequences for the rest of their lives.

It's been shown that there are some remedies to be had for Schizophrenia, however none of them treatment the underlying pathologies that result in impaired learning. Medical treatments such as medicine have been shown to have fantastic effects, but also bring their own burdens, which in flip bog down the learning process, even when used judiciously. Cognitive and psychosocial treatments within the past have no longer shown top-notch success with long-lasting adjustments. However, as we study more about the way the human-animal learns, and the outcomes of the disease, we are coming across extra methods wherein we can impact modifications for longer durations of time.

Chapter Six

Non-verbal Communication and Learning

Verbal exchange is an integral part of our lives. We communicate in exceptional ways to express our minds, emotions, know-how, talents, and ideas. It is normally assumed that conversation is recognized with speech and sounds but the conversation is, in fact, the combination of verbal and non-verbal transmission of expertise. Non-verbal communication includes sounds, gestures, body actions, eye contacts, facial expressions, pitch or tone of a voice, spatial distance, apparent behavior, postures, and get dressed person. "Language comprises all kinds of verbal exchange: crying, facial expression, gestures, touching, yelling, and additionally speech and writing." the entirety speaks within the manner of verbal exchange including cloth gadgets and physical area but handiest speech sounds or verbal manufacturing is observed, non-verbal cannot, which is a valuable factor of communique. It complements the meaning of words. A speaker can raise the interest and interest of the listeners with the assist of non-verbal verbal exchange. Extra frequently non-verbal communication happens unconsciously. Humans are not aware of the fact that besides their verbal exchange the nonverbal gestures additionally transmit a mighty message. The body language, eye contact, bodily appearance, and tone of voice provide significant data to the two target markets. Nonverbal communication is deemed tons dependable and effective in assessment to verbal communique because it offers an extra guide to the verbal exchange. For example, a mother asks her toddler, 'have you ever taken your meal?' the kid answers verbally 'yes' but nods his head and gives a message of 'No'. The mom takes the non-verbal message of the kid and ignores the verbal message. In my view, non-verbal communication is usually observed by way of children soon after their start. A child learns non-verbal expression by observing, imitating, watching, and copying other humans of the family. Kids can understand non-verbal gestures extra than verbal exchange and are extra capable of apprehending the non-verbal indicators than adults. Nonverbal communique is normally understood because of the technique of communication through sending and receiving wordless messages. i.e., language isn't always the only supply of communique, there are other means also. Nonverbal conversation can be communicated via frame actions, facial expressions, eye touch, and gestures. "A body moves, postures, or material artifacts which encodes or affects a concept, motivation, or mood (consequently, a gesture is neither depend nor power, however records). In its most popular experience is an indication, signal, or cue used to talk in tandem with, or component from phrases. Gestures encompass facial expressions, clothing cues, and frame moves".

"One of the first researchers on nonverbal communique changed into Ray Birdwhistell, who used the term "kinesics" in 1952 three while he wrote advent of Kinesics, "nonverbal communication" become used for the first time in 1955 with the aid of G.W. Hewes when he wrote world Distribution of positive Postural habits. This was accompanied by Irving Goffman's conduct in Public places which used the time period "frame idiom." That, in flip, caused Julius to speed in 1971 using the now commonplace expression "body language" inside the e-book he wrote by the same name. Mankind's expertise of nonverbal verbal exchange would have progressed further if others, except Ray Birdwhistell, had committed more time to learn the concern. At some stage in the Fifties, Birdwhistell turned into just about the simplest man or woman analyzing this method of conversation. His attempt has contributed greatly to our cutting-edge know-how and know-how of nonverbal communique." Allan and Pease (2004) said, "Albert Mehrabian, a pioneer researcher of body language in the Nineteen Fifties, found that the full impact of a message is about 7% verbal (words only) and 38% vocal (together with tone of voice, inflection, and other sounds) and 55% non-verbal." They in addition said, "Anthropologist Ray Birdwhistell pioneered the authentic have a look at of non-verbal communique-what he is known as 'Kinesics'. Birdwhistell made some similar estimates of the amount of non-verbal conversation that takes region among human beings. He anticipated that the common person honestly speaks phrases for a total of approximately ten or eleven minutes an afternoon and that the average sentence takes only 2.5 seconds. We can make and recognize around two hundred and fifty facial expressions". "Communication professionals have mounted the fact that much less than a third of the means transferred from one character to any other in a non-public conversation comes from the words which might be spoken. The general public of that means four comes from nonverbal sources, together with frame movement; eye contact; gestures; posture; and vocal tone, pitch, pacing, and phrasing. Different messages come from our apparel, our use of time, and actually dozens of other nonverbal classes. Nonverbal communique broadly seems because of the transfer of meaning without the use of verbal symbols. That is, nonverbal conversation refers in a literal sense to those actions, gadgets, and contexts that both talk without delay or facilitate communique without using words. As verbal exchange specialists and informal observers alike will testify, even though, setting apart the effects of verbal and nonverbal behavior is in no way easy, in large part because they tend to enhance each other, contradict every other, or are in a few ways approximately every different".

"While a person nods his head to signify assent (or, in some cultures, refusal), the gesture is arbitrary and therefore symbolic. Weeping is an indication of sorrow, and blushing is an indication of disgrace, but these signs and symptoms are because of the emotional states in question, and so are not arbitrary or symbolic." "People's actions often do speak louder than their phrases. In truth, the majority can misinform others lots more without difficulty with phrases than they could with their bodies. Words are relatively smooth to govern; frame language, facial expressions, and vocal traits aren't. By way of being attentive to these nonverbal cues, you could locate deception or affirm a speaker's honesty. Due to the fact nonverbal conversation is so reliable, humans usually have more religion in nonverbal cues than they do in verbal messages. If a person says one element however transmits a conflicting message nonverbally, listeners nearly forever believe 5 the nonverbal signal. Possibilities are if you can read different humans' nonverbal messages successfully, you may interpret their underlying attitudes and intentions and reply correctly". "It is important which you are heard. If you do now not reap this fundamental objective, and some speakers do not, then the whole lot else is inappropriate. You ought to adjust your voice in line with the target market and the room. If half of a dozen people are gathered in a small room, then something near a regular conversational tone will suffice. If there is a big institution of human beings you must improve your voice and challenge it." Pitch inside the voice can play a completely massive position in teaching gaining knowledge of the procedure. With the upward thrust and fall of pitch, an entire means of a phrase may be changed. Instructors can make use of this method in the know-how of the meanings of different phrases. The tone of voice displays mental arousal, emotion, and temper. It could also carry social information, as in a sarcastic, advanced, or submissive way of talking. Furthermore, proper use of tone instructors, inside the coaching of poetry is very essential and beneficial and creates hobby and curiosity among the scholars. The maximum crucial component of voice excellent to control; is pitch. Pitch refers to the highness and lowness of your voice. Consider pitch as notes on a musical scale. Simply as a melody moves up and down the scale, talking additionally uses variety in pitch to explicit which means. Naturally, your pitch is decided in component by way of your speaking voice. whether or not your voice is pretty low, high, or somewhere in between, you ought to work on growing variety within your herbal variety." inside the schoolroom setting eye contact with the teacher may be very crucial and immediately affects the overall performance of the students in addition to the lecture room control. Eye contact is a device of teaching, which a trainer may be used very correctly for the enhancement and fulfillment of college students' gaining knowledge of consequences.

The human species cost open, attractive eye contact, including is typically found in a conversation among buddies. It is subconsciously taken as a demonstration of confidence, authority, and sincerity. A smile, like a facial expression, is a powerful tool inside the palms of an instructor, that could broaden the know-how of the scholars through attracting their attention within the lecture room and creates their interest in getting to know. However anger, as a facial expression, may be used inside the study room; if college students aren't interested in the teaching gaining knowledge of the method or lose attention. Smile and anger are very powerful equipment in the fingers of a teacher, which, if used nicely and purposefully, can decorate the students' learning consequences. The gap between trainers and college students is a vital factor in the communication procedure. Instructors can effortlessly transmit feelings of recognition or rejection absolutely using the gap they hold. They have got 'freedom of area' while college students do no longer. Instructors, in addition to others, will be predisposed to get towards students they prefer. A brief remark of the lecture room will regularly identify the instructor's puppy, in addition to the one's college students, the teacher dislikes. To avoid the accusation of favoritism, instructors ought to make an aware attempt to get in the area bubble of all students. By traveling freely during the elegance, they strengthen the idea of joint ownership. The non-verbal verbal exchange performs a very massive position, inside the schoolroom, at some stage in coaching studying manner. Non-verbal conversation creates an effect on the comprehension of the scholars, which results in higher mastering and information of the principles. instructors, like each day lifestyles state of affairs, also use nonverbal conversation within the magnificence rooms however if they use it purposely and as a teaching method to create interest among the students, better results may be acquired inside the shape of college students' gaining knowledge of outcomes. Instructors can use their body moves, eye contact, facial expressions; smile; anger; frown, the pitch of voice, and distance for higher expertise of the ideas of students. Instructors can use non-verbal conversation for the fast gaining knowledge of the scholars with minimum effort. This teaching-getting-to-know process is based on getting to know goals, which in the long run ends in getting to know outcomes. These learning consequences are the stop fabricated from coaching-gaining knowledge of the method. Gaining knowledge of the results of the students and teaching-mastering procedure relies on mastering sports. The end product of all studying activities is getting to know consequences; consequently, these activities want excellent care in designing and executing in the classrooms. The better the studying sports; the high-quality may be the getting to know outcomes. Gronlund (1970) commented that there has been a relationship between gaining knowledge of manner and learning consequences. The teaching-studying procedure changed into not an end in itself but a method to a stop. Distinctive teaching methods and A.V. aids used in the eight coachings are taken into consideration as a device to acquire preferred mastering results. Getting to know consequences additionally make a contribution to academic manner in the experience that it offers a path to the academics in deciding on their teaching techniques and materials inside the lecture rooms. The gaining knowledge of sports of the scholars can be progressed inside and outside the school if learning effects are nicely communicated to them.

Communication plays a pivotal position in our everyday lives. To articulate our thoughts, emotions, feelings, and skills we talk now not best with verbal however additionally with non-verbal strategies. Those are critical in coaching-gaining knowledge of manner. Teachers can utilize a selection of verbal and non-verbal competencies to aid college students' comprehension of difficult concepts. It became an experimental have a look that regarded the impact of non-verbal communique on the mastering results of students of ninth and tenth lessons in Peshawar, Khyber Pakhtunkhwa. This look highlighted the importance of non-verbal communique inside the challenge of English (compulsory) of classes (IX-X), similarly, it explored the impact of non-verbal verbal exchange on students' studying with the aid of staring at instructors and college students in school rooms and; finding out how this mechanism contributed to higher studying consequences of students. The take a look at examining the hypotheses that there's an effect of nonverbal communication on students' getting to know results each in rural and concrete areas, and there is an effect of non-verbal verbal exchange at the studying outcomes of male and female college students. The populace of the has a look at included students and instructors of one hundred and three executives. Secondary colleges in rural and concrete regions of Peshawar. The pattern protected two teachers and forty students from each school within the challenge of English (obligatory). The total range of sample instructors and students is forty and eight hundred respectively. Tools of the data collection had been questionnaires and experiments in the real classrooms placing. The significant difference between pre and post-tests of the manipulation and experimental organizations was examined through paired t-check.

Moreover, the questionnaires have been interpreted with the help of frequency and percent ii methods, whilst the correlation among teachers and college students' questionnaires turned into performed thru Gamma correlation. The crucial conclusions indicated that instructors made the getting to know surroundings energetic thru their non-verbal verbal exchange wherein students felt alert inside the school rooms and participated inside the mastering procedure, which therefore greater the level of their retention and information. The right use of facial expressions, body moves, eye touch, the pitch of voice, and the spatial distance helped the teachers to provide a better understanding to the scholars in the attainment in their mastering outcomes. On the contrary, the academics who did not well use non-verbal communique within the lecture room could not inspire the scholars for effective learning. The look at made the subsequent pointers: 1. teachers must be given an orientation in non-verbal communique and the capabilities thus received ought to be utilized in their teaching methodologies. 2. instructors should be encouraged to apply this technology for you to initiate the hobby of the students and lead them to attentive in the elegance. 3. it's endorsed that curriculum planners and policymakers need to also apprehend the importance of non-verbal verbal exchange and make it a part of the instructor schooling program so that prospective instructors are skilled in this crucial talent.

Appropriate verbal exchange is the inspiration of successful relationships, each in my opinion and professionally. However, we communicate with lots extra than phrases. In fact, research shows that the majority of our verbal exchange is nonverbal. The sector of nonverbal communications has grown hastily over a previous couple of many years, and it has packages in commercial enterprise, media, worldwide family members, education, and indeed any field which significantly entails interpersonal and group dynamics. Surely there is a need for extra psychological mindedness in all these realms. More than three-quarters of verbal exchange is non-verbal. We all use no-verbal verbal exchange every time we talk to a person throughout the tone of our voices, our body moves, and our gestures to specific our feelings and mind. Movements speak louder than words. Instructors could realize more about their college students by watching their actions than by using being attentive to what they are saying

When we speak about the verbal exchange, we often mean

what we are saying; the phrases that we use. But, the interpersonal conversation is an awful lot extra than the specific that means of phrases, and the statistics or message that they bring about. It is also implicit messages, whether or not intentional or not, which can be expressed thru non-verbal behaviors. Non-verbal communication consists of facial expressions, the tone and pitch of the voice, gestures displayed thru frame language Kinesics) and the bodily distance between the communications (proxemics). Non-verbal alerts can deliver clues and further facts and their meaning over and above spoken (verbal) conversation. Certainly, some estimates endorse that around seventy to eighty percent of verbal exchange is non-verbal.

At the same time as the key to success in each personal and professional relationship lies in your capability to communicate properly, it's now not the words that you use but your nonverbal cues or "body language" that talk the loudest. Frame language is the usage of physical conduct, expressions, and mannerisms to communicate nonverbally, frequently achieved instinctively rather than consciously.

Whether or not you're aware of it or now not, whilst you have interaction with others, you're constantly giving and receiving wordless signals. all your nonverbal behaviors, the gestures you're making, your posture, your tone of voice, how a whole lot of eye contact you make and send robust messages. They could place humans at ease, construct trust, and draw others towards you, or they could offend, confuse, and undermine what you're seeking to bring. Those messages don't stop while you stop speaking both. Even when you're silent, you're still speaking nonverbally.

In some times, what comes from your mouth and what you communicate thru your frame language can be two definitely different things. If you say one factor, but your frame language says something else, your listener will possibly experience that you're being cheating. If you say "sure" even as shaking your head no, as an instance. Whilst faced with such blended signals, the listener has to pick out whether or not to trust your verbal or nonverbal message. Because frame language is an herbal, unconscious language that proclaims your actual feelings and intentions, they'll possibly select the nonverbal message. But, through enhancing how you recognize and use the nonverbal verbal exchange, you can express what you without a doubt imply, connect better with others, and construct stronger, greater profitable relationships.

Why does nonverbal communication depend?

Your nonverbal communication cues consist of the way you concentrate, look, flow, and react; tell the man or woman you're communicating with whether or not you care, in case you're being truthful, and the way properly you're listening. While your nonverbal alerts are healthy up with the phrases you're pronouncing, they grow trust, readability, and rapport. After they don't, they can generate tension, distrust, and confusion. If you want to end up a higher communicator, it's vital to grow to be greater touchy not simplest to the frame language and nonverbal cues of others, however additionally on your own.

Nonverbal communication can play five exceptional roles:

• Repetition: It repeats and frequently strengthens the message you're making verbally.

• Contradiction: it can contradict the message you're

trying to carry, accordingly indicating in your listener that you may now not be telling the truth.

• Substitution: it an alternative for a verbal message. as an instance, your facial expression regularly conveys a much more brilliant message than words ever can.

• Complementing: it can upload to or supplement your verbal message. As a boss, in case you placed a worker on the again similarly to giving a reward, it may boom the effect of your message.

• Accenting: it may accent or underline a verbal message. Pounding the table, as an example, can underline the significance of your message.

Types of nonverbal communique

The various unique sorts of nonverbal communique or body language encompass Facial expressions: The human face is extraordinarily expressive, able to bring endless emotions without saying a phrase. And in contrast to a few varieties of nonverbal verbal exchange, facial expressions are frequent. The facial expressions for happiness, unhappiness, anger, wonder, worry, and disgust are identical throughout cultures. Frame motion and posture: bear in mind how your perceptions of human beings are tormented by the way they take a seat, walk, stand, or preserve their head. The manner you move and deliver yourself communicates a wealth of facts to the world. This form of nonverbal communication includes your posture, bearing, stance, and the subtle movements you're making.

Gestures: Gestures are woven into the material of our daily lives. You may wave, factor, beckon or use your hands whilst arguing or talking animatedly, regularly expressing yourself with gestures without wondering. But, the means of a few gestures may be very one-of-a-kind throughout cultures. Whilst the adequate signal made with the hand, as an example, conveys a tremendous message in English-talking nations, it's kept in mind offensive in countries which include Germany, Russia, and Brazil. So, it's crucial to be careful of the way you operate gestures to avoid misinterpretation.

Eye contact: For the reason that visible experience is dominant for most people, eye touch is an especially crucial sort of nonverbal communique. The manner you examine someone can communicate much stuff, together with interest, affection, hostility, or attraction. Eye contact is likewise important in keeping the flow of verbal exchange and for gauging the other character's interest and reaction.

Touch: We speak a great deal via contact. Think about the very distinctive messages given via a weak handshake, a heat bear hug, a patronizing pat on the head, or a controlling grip at the arm, for example.

Space: Have you ever felt uncomfortable at some point in a communique due to the fact the alternative man or woman was standing too close and invading your space? We all need bodily space, even though that want differs depending on the way of life, the scenario, and the closeness of the relationship. You may use the physical area to communicate many special nonverbal messages, which include signals of intimacy and affection, aggression, or dominance.

Voice: It's not just what you are saying, it's the way you say it. While you speak, different human beings "read" your voice further to being attentive to your words. Matters they pay attention to include your timing and tempo, how loud you talk, your tone and inflection, and sounds that bring information, inclusive of "ahh" and "uh-huh." reflect on consideration on how your tone of voice can imply sarcasm, anger, affection, or confidence.

Effective nonverbal communique

Regardless of their significance, words are not the handiest way that instructors and students communicate. Gestures and behaviors bring records as nicely, often helping a trainer's words, but on occasion also contradicting them. Students and teachers specific themselves nonverbally in all conversations, so freely and mechanically in reality that this form of communication can without difficulty be ignored.

Eye touch

One critical nonverbal conduct is eye touch, which is the volume and timing of while a speaker appears immediately in the eyes of the listener. In conversations among buddies of identical reputation, as an instance, maximum native speakers of English tend to appear at once on the speaker while listening, however, to prevent their gaze when speaking. Re-enticing eye contact, in truth, frequently alerts that a speaker is about to finish a flip and is inviting a response from the listener.

However, conversations observe unique rules if they involve someone of greater authority talking with someone of lesser authority, consisting of among a trainer and a scholar. If so, the man or woman in authority signals greater status using looking directly at the listener almost constantly, whether or not listening or speaking. This exchange sample can now and again prove awkward if both parties aren't waiting for it. for college students' unused to non-stop eye contact, it could experience like the teacher is staring excessively, intrusively, or inappropriately; an ironic effect maybe for the scholar to feel extra self-aware instead of more engaged, as intended. For similar motives, inexperienced or first-time teachers also can experience uncomfortable with looking at college students constantly. Although studies about the consequences of eye contact indicate that it can assist all people, whether or not a scholar or trainer, to don't forget what they may be seeing and listening to.

Conversation troubles result much less from eye touch as such than from differences in expectations approximately eye contact. If college students' expectancies range a very lot from the instructor's, one birthday party may misinterpret the other celebration's motivations. Among some non-white ethnic organizations, as an example, eye contact follows a sample that reverses the traditional white, English-language sample: they generally tend to look more closely at a companion while speaking, and forestall gaze whilst listening. The alternative pattern works flawlessly properly so long as both events assume it and use it. As you may think, although, there are issues if the two partners use contrary patterns of eye contact. In that case, one person may also interpret an immediate gaze as an invitation to begin speaking, whilst definitely, it's miles an invitation to forestall speaking. Sooner or later the conversational companion might also locate himself interrupting an excessive amount of, or truly talking too lengthy at a flip. They speak also can happen: if the first person seems away, the companion may take the gesture as inviting the partner to maintain listening, whilst virtually the first individual is inviting the companion to start speaking. Awkward gaps among comments may additionally result. In either case, if the conversational partners are a teacher and scholar, rapport may deteriorate step by step. Inside the first case, the trainer may additionally even finish, wrongly, that the student is socially inept due to the fact the scholar interrupts a lot. Inside the second case, the teacher can also conclude—also wrongly—that the scholar may be very shy or maybe lacking in language skills.

To avoid such misunderstandings, a teacher wishes to observe and consider students' favored gaze styles at times when students are loose to look anywhere and at whomever they please. traditional seats-in-a-row desk preparations do no longer work nicely for this cause; as you may suppose, and as research confirms, sitting in rows makes college students much more likely to appear either at the trainer or to examine not anything in particular. Almost every other seating association, which includes sitting in clusters or a circle, encourages freer styles of eye contact. more cozy eye contact, in flip, makes for verbal exchange this is greater cozy and efficient.

Wait time

Another essential nonverbal behavior is the wait time, which's the pause among conversational turns. Wait time marks when a conversational turn starts or ends. If a trainer asks a query, for instance, the wait time each lets in and activates students to formulate the best reaction. Research on study room interplay normally shows that wait instances in most classes are remarkably short, much less than one second. Sadly wait times this quick can virtually intervene with most college students' questioning; in a single second, maximum students either cannot determine what to mention or can most effectively don't forget an easy, computerized truth. Growing wait instances to numerous seconds have numerous desirable results: students supply longer, more complex responses, they express extra complex thoughts, and a much broader variety of college students participate in the dialogue. for plenty of instructors, but, mastering to increase wait time this lots takes conscious effort and may feel uncomfortable at the start. A trick is, if you are attempting to wait longer, is to rely silently on earlier than calling on each person. After a few weeks of exercise, soreness with longer wait times usually subsides, and the educational benefits of waiting emerge as more obvious.

As with eye touch, desired wait instances vary both among people and amongst businesses of college students, and the differences in expected wait times can sometimes result in awkward conversations. although there are numerous exceptions, ladies tend to select longer wait times than boys—perhaps contributing to an impact that ladies are unnecessarily shy or that boys are self-focused or impulsive. College students from a few ethnic and cultural groups tend to decide on miles longer wait time than is typical to be had in a lecture room, especially while English is the scholar's second language. Whilst a trainer converses with a member of any such organization, therefore, what feels to the pupil like a respectful pause can also appear to be hesitation or resistance to the teacher. Yet other cultural companies certainly opt for overlapping feedback—a kind of bad wait time. In those situations, one conversational associate will begin at precisely the equal immediate because of the previous speaker, or maybe earlier than the speaker has completed. The bad wait time is meant to signal energetic hobbies in the communique. An instructor who is used to a one-second gap among feedback, but, can also regard overlapping remarks as impolite interruptions, and may additionally have trouble getting probabilities to speak.

Even though longer wait instances are frequently most desirable, they do now not constantly work nicely with certain people or organizations. For teachers, the most broadly beneficial recommendation is to healthy wait time to the students' alternatives as closely as possible, irrespective of whether these are slower or quicker than what the teacher normally prefers. To the quantity that a teacher and students can match every other's pace, they'll communicate greater without problems and completely, and a bigger percentage of college students will take part in discussions and sports. As with eye contact, staring at college students' favored wait times is easier in situations that supply college students some degree of freedom about while and the way to participate, such as open-ended discussions or informal conversations at some stage in the day.

Social distance

Whilst humans have interaction, the bodily area or distance among them, their social distance often suggests something approximately how intimate or non-public their dating is. Social distance also impacts how human beings describe others and their actions; someone who habitually is more remote physically is apt to be described in more well-known, summary phrases than someone who regularly strategies greater closely. In white American society, a distance of about half a meter to a meter is what most people pick while speaking face-to-face with a personal buddy. The closer quit of this variety is extra, not unusual if the individuals flip sideways to each other, as when driving on an elevator; but typically the nearest distances are reserved for genuinely intimate friendships, such as between spouses. If the relationship is extra businesslike, individuals are much more likely to situate themselves inside the range of about one meter to three meters. This is a commonplace distance, for instance, for a trainer speaking with a student or speaking with a small group of college students. For nevertheless greater formal interactions, individuals generally tend to allow more than three meters; this distance is traditional, for instance, whilst a trainer speaks to an entire elegance.

Simply as with eye contact and wait time, however, individuals differ within the distances they prefer for those exclusive levels of intimacy, and headaches happen if two human beings assume special distances for the same form of dating. A scholar who prefers a shorter social distance than her companion can seem pushy or overly acquainted with the associate. The latter, in turn, can appear aloof or unfriendly—actually "remote." The sources of those results are smooth to overlook considering that by definition the companions never discuss social distance verbally, but they're real. The first-class treatment, once more, is for instructors to study college students' evidently going on options as intently as possible, and to appreciate them as plenty as feasible: students who need to be closer must be allowed to be nearer, at least inside reasonable limits, and those who want to be greater remote ought to be allowed to be extra remote.

Chapter Seven

Attitude, Personality, and Learning

Psychologists outline attitudes as a learned tendency to evaluate things positively. This may consist of evaluations of people, problems, gadgets, or activities. Such opinions are often fantastic or bad, but they can also be unsure in instances. For example, you might have blended feelings about a particular man or woman or issue. Researchers also endorse that there are several exclusive components that makeup attitudes. The components of attitudes are sometimes known as CAB or the ABC's of mindset.
Components of attitude:
• Cognitive aspect: Your mind and beliefs approximately the challenge.
• Affective aspect: How the item, person, issue, or event makes you feel.
• Behavioural element: How mindset influences your behavior.

Attitudes also can be express and implicit. Express attitudes are people who we're consciously privy to and that definitely have an impact on our behaviors and ideals. Implicit attitudes are subconscious but affect our beliefs and behaviors.
Attitude Formation
There are a variety of factors that can have an impact on

how and why attitudes form. Right here is a better take a look at how attitudes form. Attitudes form without delay due to revel in. they'll emerge due to direct private experience, or they may result from commentary. Social roles and social norms can have a robust effect on attitudes. Social roles relate to how people are expected to act in a selected position or context. Social norms involve society's regulations for what behaviors are taken into consideration appropriately.

Mastering

Attitudes can be discovered in a spread of ways. Don't forget how advertisers use classical conditioning to persuade your attitude in the direction of a particular product. In a television business, you notice younger, stunning human beings having a laugh on a tropical seaside whilst playing a sports activities drink. This attractive and attractive imagery causes you to broaden a fine affiliation with this precise beverage. Operant conditioning can also be used to steer how attitudes broaden. Believe a younger man who has just started smoking. On every occasion he lighting up a cigarette, human beings bitch, chastise him and ask him to depart their location. These terrible comments from those around him eventually reason him to increase a detrimental opinion of smoking and he decides to give up the addiction. Eventually, humans additionally analyze attitudes by looking at people around them. When a person you recognize greatly espouses a selected mindset, you're more likely to broaden the equal beliefs. As an instance, children spend a fantastic deal of time observing the attitudes of their dad and mom and commonly start to exhibit similar outlooks. We generally tend to anticipate that human beings behave in keeping with their attitudes. But, social psychologists have discovered that attitudes and actual behavior aren't constantly perfectly aligned. In the end, lots of people guide a particular candidate or political birthday celebration and yet fail to exit and vote. Human beings are also more likely to act in step with their attitudes beneath sure situations.

Elements influencing mindset energy

- Is a professional on the challenge
- Count on a beneficial outcome
- experience something for my part
- Stand to win or lose something because of the problem
- Are repeatedly expressed attitudes

Changing to healthy conduct

In some instances, human beings may additionally clearly modify their attitudes with a view to higher align them with their conduct. Cognitive dissonance is a phenomenon wherein someone stories mental distress because of conflicting thoughts or ideals. To lessen this tension, human beings might also trade their attitudes to mirror their other ideals or actual behaviors.

The usage of cognitive dissonance

Believe the subsequent scenario: you've got always located an excessive price on monetary security, however you begin dating someone who's very financially unstable. On the way to lessen the tension due to the conflicting beliefs and conduct, you have got alternatives. You may give up the relationship and are searching for a companion who's more financially cozy, or you can de-emphasize monetary balance significance. So that you can reduce the dissonance between your conflicting mindset and behavior, you either have to trade the attitude or trade your action. At the same time as attitudes will have an effective impact on conduct, they may be not set in stone. The identical effects that cause mindset formation can also create mindset alternations.

Studying theory

Classical conditioning, operant conditioning, and observational getting to know may be used to result in attitude trade. Classical conditioning may be used to create high-quality emotional reactions to an item, individual, or occasion using associating positive feelings with the goal item. Operant conditioning can be used to reinforce desirable attitudes and weaken unwanted ones. Human beings can also trade their attitudes after observing the conduct of others.

Elaboration likelihood concept

This principle of persuasion indicates that people can regulate their attitudes in approaches. First, they can be influenced to pay attention and consider the message, therefore main to a mindset shift.

Or, they might be stimulated via the characteristics of the speaker, leading to a brief or surface shift in attitude. Messages which might be notion-scary and that enchantment to common sense are much more likely to lead to everlasting adjustments in attitudes.

Dissonance principle

As referred to in advance, human beings can also change their attitudes when they have conflicting ideas about a subject. To reduce the anxiety created using these incompatible ideals, humans regularly shift their attitudes.

The character has been identified as being an essential contributing component in the improvement of students' attitude towards Chemistry. The purpose of modern observation is to take a look at the influence of persona on students' mindset in the direction of Chemistry. The study additionally determines the impact of Age, Gender, family kind, elegance, school area, Father Qualification, mom Qualification, preference Of route on students' character, and affective characteristics of attitude. Only a few types of research have dealt with this dimension of training in Pakistan. The populace of the look at constructed from Secondary colleges male and woman students. Gadgets used for records series become advanced using the researcher reliability became first tested via pilot testing. Records were analyzed by using the use of Correlation, t-check, and analysis of Variance (ANOVA). It w concluded from the observation that the two factors are interrelated Character is hard and fast of a consistent and specific pattern of thoughts, feelings, and behavior that makes human beings one of a kind from each other .personality means how human beings recognize themselves and their surroundings. Character no longer handiest have an impact on how to reply in our surroundings; additionally are expecting to behave surely.

Pervin (1996) describes personality as a complicated corporation of cognitions, influences, and behaviors that give direction and pattern to the man or woman's existence.

Exceptional strategies to personality

- The Behavioral technique

Skinner's view is frequently termed radical behaviorism

because of his insistence on referring to environmental occasions in considering any behavior. Character is based only on discovered conduct and contingencies of reinforcement. He also believes that internal events inclusive of thoughts or feelings are outcomes of external activities, not reasons for them. The central recognition of the Behavioral approach, elaborated via Bandura and others, is on the system of modeling, the remark of a few other individual's actions, and the learning from those moves., without the observer always both appearing the motion or being rewarded for it. Behavioral technique sees a person's character as growing via an entire life interplay among the individual and his or her environment, each of which affects the opposite. It gives a bendy framework for combining self and state of affairs variables, including cognitive functions

- The Humanistic technique

The humanistic technique is generally attributed to the impartial strategies of two theorists, Abraham Maslow, and Carl Rogers. Each emphasizes principles of the self and self-improvement, but they vary truly in how those concepts are described and used. Maslow saw weak, innate, high-quality inclinations that must be nurtured. Survival reasons are the maximum power and most on-the-spot motives. Maslow proposed his famous hierarchy of wishes to suggest how more solely human needs would possibly appear after extra basic wishes were happy. in keeping with Maslow, all the needs inside the hierarchy are innate to human beings, but the ones better in the hierarchy are weaker; they handiest direct motion when all earlier wishes have been glad. Roger's view is worried about the development of self, however he tactics the idea of self in a different way than Maslow did. Roger's character concept is a person-targeted theory in several ways. Roger's view is character-focused in emphasizing self-actualization. Consistent with Rogers, self-actualizing is to strive toward equivalence among one's concept of self and one's enjoyment. Roger's theory is consequently an aggregate of emotional and cognitive elements.

• The Trait method to personality

One of the maximum first-rate trait psychologists changed into Gordon Allport. A psychological Interpretation launched the psychology of a character as a discipline and discipline. In his classic work and lots of later contributions, he made a convincing case that an exclusive subject turned into wished, to understand the person as a coherent, steady whole individual. His view of personality turned wide and integrative. Reacting in opposition to the tendency of researchers to examine remote part tactics, along with getting to know and memory, in methods that did not take account of man or woman differences, he wanted to pursue goals. One became to apprehend the differences between humans in character; the alternative turned into to see how the unique characteristics that exist within a man or woman have interaction and feature collectively in an included way. Allport (1937), in his concept, explains that trends have a very actual life: they're the last realities of mental organization.

Traits are highly fashionable and enduring: they unite many responses to various stimuli, producing pretty wide consistencies in behavior. It's far believed that some humans have tendencies that impact most components in their conduct. He called these highly generalized tendencies cardinal traits. For instance, if someone's complete life appears to be prepared around goal achievement and the attainment of excellence, then fulfillment is probably his or her cardinal trait. Much less pervasive but quite generalized dispositions are crucial tendencies, and Allport thought that many humans are widely motivated with the aid of important trends. Finally, more precise, slim tendencies are referred to as secondary dispositions or "attitudes". It's also said that one's sample of inclinations or "persona shape" determines one's behavior. No two human beings are absolutely alike, and therefore no two human beings reply identically to the equal occasion. All of our behavior is decided by a selected trait structure.

Big five persona trait

The five-component version of persona is a corporation of personality developments in phrases of five primary dimensions which includes the subsequent character additives: Extraversion refers to the tendency to opt for social interplay. Extraverted people are socially lively, amusing-loving, and generally tend to take group leadership positions. Extraverts tend to be talkative, social, gregarious, and assertive, and revel in fine outcomes along with strength, zeal, and exhilaration, and the tendency to decide upon social interaction. Extroverted human beings are socially lively, laugh-loving, and tend to take group leadership positions.

Neuroticism refers to the tendency to enjoy bad emotions including melancholy and anxiety. It consists of the tendency to be temperamental and sense prone. Therefore, a high level of neuroticism probably leads to emotional instability and frustration. Neuroticism represents the tendency to exhibit terrible emotional adjustment and revel in terrible effects along with anxiety, insecurity, and hostility. Neurotic individuals are more prone to psychological misery and usually cope more poorly with misery than others.

Openness to experience includes preference and popularity of the latest thoughts and experiences. It reflects creativity, imagination, and liberalism." Openness is the disposition to be creative, unconventional, and self-reliant. People with exquisite Openness to reviews are conscious of and curious about each they're inner and outer international. The tendency to be cooperative, compassionate, and good-natured is endorsed through agreeable humans who tend to avoid interpersonal struggle. In comparison, humans with low agreeableness are probably aggressive, crucial suspicious, and impatient. Openness to experience is the tendency in the direction of being imaginative, open to new reviews, and having a vast range of hobbies.

Agreeableness refers to the tendency to be cooperative, compassionate, and true-natured. Agreeable humans generally tend to keep away from interpersonal war. In assessment, human beings with low agreeableness are possibly competitive, important, suspicious, and impatient. Agreeableness is the tendency to be trusting, compliant, being concerned, and mild. Agreeable people are commonly suitable-natured, cooperative, supportive, caring, and concerned for others. They usually believe and trust that others are honest and well-intentioned.

Conscientiousness refers back to the tendency to be self-disciplined, aim-orientated, and formidable. Conscientious human beings are prepared and feature self-efficacy and endurance. the ones without conscientiousness are easygoing, impulsive, and careless. The tendency to be self-disciplined, aim-oriented, and bold is the trait of conscientious humans who are prepared and have self-efficacy and endurance. The ones without conscientiousness are easygoing, impulsive, and careless. Conscientiousness is produced from two associated facets: achievement and dependability, and Conscientiousness has been located to be the essential issue of integrity. Conscientious people are likely to be dependable, accountable, rule-abiding, and achievement-orientated.

Attitude

Attitude is one of the most important standards in social psychology. From a behavioral view, mindset is described as an "intellectual and neural kingdom of readiness to reply, organized through revel in, exerting a directive and/or dynamic impact upon the man or woman's response to all items and conditions with which it's far associated. In other phrases, attitudes are considered as dispositions or predispositions to respond to sure stimuli, and the traditional tripartite version incorporates three important styles of responses: cognitive, affective, and behavioral. Attitude can be described because of the emotions that a person has about an item, primarily based on his or her understanding and belief approximately that item. This definition is made based on the model that attitudes include the three components of cognition, affect on, and behavior. Social psychologists have additionally long regarded attitudes as having three components.

A conceptual framework for mind-set

The cognitive aspect is a set of ideals approximately the

attributes of the attitudes. The Behavioral element relates to the way humans act in the direction of the object. The Affective aspect includes feelings approximately item i.e., the thoughts and feelings one has towards a mindset item consisting of chemistry lessons and chemistry concern are referred to the as effective factor of view. We will say "affect" pertains to how people sense the object (both appropriate and awful feelings), as expressed via physiological pastime or overt conversation. Affective characteristics are as a great deal crucial as cognitive variables in influencing learning consequences, profession picks, and use of enjoyment time. Affective traits include in this examination are: Motivation, additionally called academic engagement, refers to "cognitive, emotional, and behavioral indicators of student investment in and attachment to schooling.

Gredler, Broussard, and Garrison (2004) outline motivation as "the characteristic that moves us to do or no longer to do something". Turner (1995) considers motivation to be synonymous with cognitive engagement, which he defines as "voluntary uses of high-stage self-regulated mastering techniques, including paying interest, connection, planning, and tracking". Consistent with Gardner and Tamir (1989a) 'interest' commonly refers to the choice to interact in a few varieties of sports in place of others. Interest may seem like an extraordinarily specific kind of mindset: while we're interested in a particular phenomenon or pastime, we are favorably willing to take care of it and provide time to it. Pastimes boom while students experience ready, so although college students aren't initially interested in a topic or pastime, they may broaden pastimes as they enjoy fulfillment.

Spielberger (1983) described tension as "The subjective feeling of anxiety, apprehension, nervousness, and worry associated with an arousal of the automated anxious system". Anxiety isn't a pathological situation in itself however a vital and normal physiological and intellectual coaching for threat,¦ anxiety is important for the survival of the man or woman underneath positive instances. Failure to recognize chance and to put together for it can have disastrous effects". Entertainment is an emotion. it is about how we sense, now not approximately what we suppose'. Psychologists have described amusement as an affective country of pleasure. Students' attitudes modifications across grade levels in terms of "entertainment of chemistry" constructs. moreover, the in-intensity evaluation indicated that there are substantial implied differences among Grade nine and Grade ten college students' attitudes toward chemistry as a college situation on leisure dimensions. The mindset literature introduced also studies associated with college students' amusement of technology instructions. Absolutely, enjoyment of chemistry, physics, or biology changed into associated with gender variations in most of the studies. Stables (1990) found that women have a propensity to organic sciences and adult males to physical sciences, and Whitfield (1979) pronounced chemistry and physics because of the least enjoyable subjects for put up fourteen English students.

The majority of college students recognize that chemistry knowledge is beneficial to interpret factors in their normal existence, however only four% of college students explicit their desire to hold chemistry studies. Achievement motivation has been described because of the extent to which people range in their want to strive to obtain rewards, including bodily pleasure, praise from others, and emotions of personal mastery.

Persona, Attitudes, Values, and Motivation

A character's effectiveness within the place of business or at school frequently depends on his/her character, attitudes, and values, alongside along with his/her motivation to prevail. Simultaneously, the belief, attitudes, and values of affiliates play a position in determining the character's effectiveness. Understanding these characteristics of employees and students can be very critical for businesses to function effectively. At the same time, it's miles critical that they apprehend the values related to the business enterprise so that it will avoid any conflicting feelings in the direction of the work they're assigned to do. By recognizing and appreciating each different trait and constraint, personnel and the companies they may be a part of, form an enormously useful.

In current years, I have realized that individuals portray similar traits; he is powerful, fast-paced, constantly desires his way, and receives frustration if he cannot acquire his desires, however still is familiar with others' emotions and attempts to make up for his mistakes. But, I realized that such persona tendencies are not best on this, and over the last few years, I have taken to aggressively pursuing my goals, no matter being pushed for time. I nonetheless do get annoyed once I do no longer achieve my dreams, but I do not worry about how others view me and therefore, have lost a chunk of the ability to feel others' feelings and feelings. In greater general phrases, I believe that heredity has truly played a crucial role in presenting me with power and aggressiveness to pursue my dreams and influencing my reflexes, power level, and biological rhythm. However, concurrently, many aspects of my persona have been molded thru my very own revel in and my want to reap what I purpose for. From a completely young age, I've evolved a character which is aggressively involved "in a chronic, incessant conflict to acquire increasingly more in much less and much less time and, if essential, in opposition to the opposing efforts of different matters or other human beings", which I've come to find out, is called a type-A character.

Character vs attitude

Many use personality and mindset as interchangeable words, while in reality, they have got completely distinctive meanings. Personality is the visible aspect of one's man or woman because it impresses others. Attitude is way, disposition, and emotions in regards to someone. Character as defined with the aid of the Oxford English Dictionary is the combination of traits or traits that form a character's specific person. Personalities are in general strong. You may not be able to pass round and alternate absolutely everyone's personality you run into. To sum up persona into five words, I would use "we are who we are". An instance that I assume is going remarkable to clarify the distinction between character and attitude is when human beings mix up Spider-guy. Spider-guy is an extremely good hero who's destined to shop the arena from his evil nemeses. Peter Parker is the regular guy below the mask. He's quite exclusive from Spider-guy. Peter Parker's personality is to assist anyone and store the sector. But to his archenemies, he can come off as impolite as he is attempting to wreck them. His mindset towards them is unfriendly. Then again attitude is described as, a settled way of questioning or feeling approximately a person or something, usually one this is pondered in a person's behavior. Your attitude may additionally range differently primarily based on extraordinary individuals. Your mindset represents your likes or dislikes for a certain idea or a given situation. Mindset will adjust with distinct situations and reports. Whilst human beings say they want to come to be higher humans, they're not making plans to change their persona, they need to change their attitudes due to the fact their attitudes impact their conduct. On studies among nature vs nurture controversy, they indicated that approximately center of the paper, they have advised that three major components form a mindset: emotional, cognitive, and behavioral. The way you sense approximately the concern, your mind and ideals the situation, and the way the attitude influences your behavior. Researchers have also determined out that attitudes may be express or implicit. Explicit attitudes are those which might be obvious and we are consciously aware of them. Implicit attitudes are unconscious, but they nonetheless play a role on how our perception and mindset. In end, thru many life stories, I've learned that there are multiple differences between persona and attitude. The principal difference between character and attitude is personality is just like a person while mindset is feeling about something. Character is the traits of a man or woman whilst their attitudes are their method to a selected idea.

What determines our persona?

Our character is defined as a fixed of tendencies that may provide an explanation for or expect a person's behavior in the diffusion of situations. In different words, personality is a set of characteristics that mirror the manner we suppose and act in a given scenario. Because of this, our personality has loads to do with how we relate to one another at work. How we assume, what we experience, and our everyday conduct signifies what our colleagues come to anticipate folks each in behavior and the expectancy of their interactions with us. For example, permits assume at work you are recognized for being on time however unexpectedly start showing up late day by day. This immediately conflicts along with your character—this is, the reality in which you are conscientious. As a result, coworkers would possibly start to accept something as true with something wrong. On the other hand, if you did no longer have this characteristic, it might not be as sudden or noteworthy. Likewise, in case your generally even-tempered supervisor yells at you for something minor, you may accept as true with there's something more to his or her anger in view that this isn't an everyday character trait and additionally may have a more difficult time coping with the situation because you didn't expect it. Whilst we come to expect a person to act a positive way, we learn how to have interact with them primarily based on their character. This goes with each method, and people discover ways to engage with us based totally on our persona. Whilst we behave exclusively than our everyday persona tendencies, human beings may take time to adjust to the state of affairs.

Personality additionally influences our ability to interact

with others, which could affect our career fulfillment. In a 2009 look, it was found that the personality function of neuroticism (a bent to enjoy bad emotional states) had a greater impact than any persona feature on figuring out future career success. In different phrases, people with nice and hopeful personalities tend to be rewarded via professional success later in life.

Even though there may be debate among whether or not or now not our personalities are inherent whilst we are born (nature) versus the manner we grew up (nurture), most researchers agree that character is mostly a result of each nature and our environmental/education studies. As an example, you've got possibly heard someone say, "She acts similar to her mother." She probably behaves that way because she became born with a number of her mom's developments, in addition to because she found out some of the behaviors her mother handed to her whilst growing up.

Nature and nurture elements determine our personality

Any other instance might be a person who grows up with their parents continuously having events. As a result, as a person, this individual may additionally become organizing loads of parties, too. Or the influence of parties may also create the opposite effect, in which the man or woman doesn't need to have events in any respect. Environmental and educational studies can create fantastic or terrible associations, which result in how we sense approximately any state of affairs that occurs in our lives. Our character: Is It Genetically Inherited or determined through the Environmental factors?

Our values assist determine our character. Our values are the ones matters we find maximum importance to us. As an example, in case your price is calm and peaceful, your character might display this in many possible methods. You might favor having some close pals and avoid going to a nightclub on Saturday nights. You may pick out a less demanding career direction, and you may find it hard to work in an area where the common battle happens.

We often locate ourselves in conditions in which our values do now not coincide with someone we are running with. For example, if Alison's primary fee is a connection, this can come out in a warm conversation fashion with coworkers and a hobby of their private lives. Imagine Alison works with Tyler, whose middle value is performance. Because of Tyler's cognizance, he can also discover it a waste of time to make small speak with colleagues. Whilst Alison approaches Tyler and asks about his weekend, she may also experience angry or disappointment while he brushes her off to invite approximately the mission they're operating on collectively. She looks like a connection wasn't made, and he looks like she isn't efficient. Expertise in our very own values in addition to the values of others can significantly help us end up higher communicators.

What are approximately our attitudes?

Our attitudes are favorable or damaging opinions in the direction of people, matters, or conditions. Many stuff affects our attitudes, including the surroundings we were added up in and our personal stories. Our personalities and values play a huge function in our attitudes as well. As an instance, many people can also have attitudes in the direction of politics that might be similar to their mother and father, but their attitudes may additionally exchange as they benefit from extra experiences. If someone has a horrific enjoyment round the ocean, they will broaden a terrible attitude around seaside sports. But, count on that man or woman has a memorable experience seeing sea lions on the beach, as an instance, then she or he can also alternate their opinion approximately the sea. Likewise, a person may additionally have cherished the ocean, but if they have a frightening enjoyment, which includes almost drowning, they will change their mindset.

The critical issue to consider approximately attitudes is that they can trade over time, but normally some type of positive enjoy desires to occur for our attitudes to alternate dramatically for the better. We also have control of our attitude in our thoughts. If we constantly circulation a terrible mind, we may also come to be a negative man or woman.

In a workplace environment, you could see where the mindset is vital. Someone's persona may be pleased and upbeat. These are the prized personnel due to the fact they help convey high-quality perspective to the place of the job. Likewise, a person with a bad mindset is generally someone that the general public opts for now not to work with. The trouble with a bad mindset is that it has a devastating effect on anybody else. Have you ever felt honestly satisfied after a terrific day and while you purchased home, your roommate was in a horrible temper because of her terrible day? In this situation, you could nearly sense you're self-deflating! That is why having a wonderful mindset is a key aspect to having exact human relations at work and in our non-public lives.

However, how do we exchange a bad mindset? Because a bad mindset can come from many resources, there also are many sources that may help us improve our mindset. "Converting your mindset" points out that our mindset is ultimately about how we set our expectations; how we manage the scenario whilst our expectations aren't met; and subsequently, how we sum up an enjoyment, individual, or situation. When we cognizance of improving our mindset on an everyday foundation, we get used to thinking definitely and our entire personality can alternate. It goes without saying that employers prefer to lease and sell a person with a wonderful mindset in preference to a bad one. Enhancing mindset includes:

• Be conscious of your bad thoughts. Hold a journal of terrible mind. Upon reviewing them, analyze why you had a negative idea approximately a specific situation.

• Try to keep away from negative wondering. Think of a stop register the thoughts that prevent you if you have poor thoughts. Try to show those thoughts into advantageous ones. For instance, in place of announcing, "I'm horrible in math," say, "I didn't do properly on that check. It just approaches I will examine harder next time."

• Spend time with high-quality humans. Everybody probably has a pal who continually seems to be negative or a coworker who continuously complains. People like this can negatively affect our mindset, too, so steerage clean while viable, or restricting the interaction time, is a first-rate manner to maintain an advantageous mindset intact.

• Spend time in a relaxed physical environment. If your bed isn't relaxed and also you aren't getting sufficient sleep, it's far extra difficult to have a superb mindset! Or if the mild on your office is simply too darkish, it is probably extra difficult to sense high-quality approximately the day. Being a hit learner starts with having a tremendous mindset toward mastering an advantageous mindset helps you to loosen up, consider, cognizance, and take in information as you research. You're prepared to welcome new stories and apprehend many extraordinary kinds of getting to know possibilities. And whilst you can see opportunities, your wish will increase. Take Eileen, for instance. Eileen has recently enrolled in university, even though it's been two decades due to the fact she wrote a paper or studied for an examination. However, in the fifteen years that she has stayed home to elevate her children, Eileen has mastered stress and time control abilities, teamwork talents, budgeting skills, and more. She has evolved online abilities, read plenty, chaired community committees, and coached several football teams. Based totally on her experience, she knows she can polish up her document writing and examine talents, and do nicely in her software. Do you stay open to studying opportunities? Do you trust which you're capable of study new things?

Use this exercise to discover your attitudes and ideals approximately mastering. Placed a checkmark beside the statements that are authentic for you:

• I trust lifelong getting to know will help me achieve my dreams.

• I am willing to make errors and examine them.

• I am conscious that getting to know opportunities are all around me.

• I take a fee for my own learning. I use each opportunity I need to learn something new.

• I'm inclined and eager to analyze.

- I realize what skills and expertise I want or need to research.
- I recognize where to find out about formal mastering opportunities thru mentors, co-workers, pals, supervisors, family participants, and my personal research.
- I set new getting to know dreams regularly.

How many did you rate out of eight viable check marks? Take a near have a look at the statements you failed to check off. Think about how these attitudes may be affecting your fulfillment as a learner. For every assertion which you didn't test off, think of two steps that you may take proper now to construct a fantastic studying mindset in this area. For instance, in case you do not know what abilities and information you want to research, how can you find out? In case you're working, may want to you ask your supervisor?

Studying opportunities

Formal school room mastering can be critical and precious, but it is the most effective one of many learning possibilities that are open to you. You can learn:

- At work
- For your personal
- From mentors and function models
- From co-employees and friends
- Online by using search engines like Google, following blogs, downloading podcasts, taking a category, and so on.
- Via magazines, journals, newspapers, motion pictures, broadcasts
- Through volunteering
- With the aid of teaching others what you understand, which allows you to enhance your abilities and perception
- Through seminars, workshops, and courses

• Via attending lessons at an educational group, in individual or online

The role of mindset in teaching

The classroom is a place wherein children flock to examine new things, and it can be a piece loopy now and then. As an instructor, you need to continue to be superb and robust-willed. Mindset may be very important whilst you are a trainer. It affects your college students in many ways and can form their gaining knowledge of enjoying. It is a reality that teachers can't clearly fool students, so it's quality now not to try, college students can and do sense instructor's moods and attitudes.

As an instructor, you'll now and again experience strain that carries with you all of the way domestic. In place of residing on this, discover effective methods to get rid of your pressure. Complaining about how bad your day was won't make the following day better. So, see what went wrong and attempt to turn it around. Did it disappoint you when your college students didn't do the analysis? Have been you frustrated along with your kindergarteners due to the fact they were extra rowdy that day? Instead of specializing in what went incorrect, prepare yourself for tomorrow, emotionally, mentally, and bodily.

Similarly, a further hour of sleep can drastically improve your temper as well as a few motivational phrases or a devotional analysis. Additionally, don't take it personally when your college students don't do the homework or whilst your college students determine to speak over you. Staying cool, calm, and amassed will allow you to properly and in reality think of a reasonable answer in place of lashing out. It is also essential to assist college students to remember that it's miles ok to have a terrible day occasionally. Instructors are just as human as their college students and can find it not possible to go a whole school year without having at least one terrible day.

The energy of positivity

The awesome aspect approximately positivity is that it doesn't simply affect one place of your existence. It affects every area. Relying on your personality and your upbringing, you could now not consider that your happiness subjects.

But the happier you are, the extra you lean into the high-quality version of yourself. This creates a ripple impact—when you're full of pleasure and peace, you emerge as a better student, a higher friend, and a better teacher.

Positivity makes it less complicated to acquire your desires. That's due to the fact while you're in a fine body of thoughts, you could make higher selections. You could appearance beforehand and plot a route, rather than just reacting to the setbacks you come across. You don't get caught with poor self-communicate. Right here are reminders about the significance of a superb mindset for students.

It's additionally less complicated to invite for assist while you're feeling advantageous. This means when you see an obstacle in your direction, you're much more likely to reach out to a trainer or parent for a recommendation. Soaking of their wisdom may be simply what you need to conquer your impediment and find fulfillment.

Positivity can even enhance your fitness.

One manner that positivity can increase your fitness is by reducing your blood pressure and coronary heart fee. Whilst you're experiencing bad feelings like anger or worry, your body will start producing adrenaline, the flight-or-combat hormone. This is a superb mechanism whilst you're confronted with an emergency like a severe vehicle twist of fate or residence fire. However, when you're faced with something much less intense like turning a paper or taking an examination, that adrenaline reaction just isn't useful. Luckily, positivity makes it less difficult to relax and manage pressure, so you don't should spend the day feeling like you're on a rollercoaster.

Positivity increases your pride in existence and college

It's clean for students (and adults) to get centered on everything incorrect in the world and it's tempting to spend it slow searching at what all of us else has. But all of that wishing and jealousy is just another shape of negativity. When you pick out to embody superb mind and attention on the stuff you're thankful for and a hit at, you forestall comparing yourself. Rather, you may see all of the top-notch things around you—like your instructors, buddies, and circle of relatives.

Positivity enables you to grow

Positivity can be useful by way of prompting students to take risks and strive for new matters inside the schoolroom and at domestic. for instance, college students might experiment with taking trumpet instructions and find out that they love the device or they might strive running and find they're new favored exercising ordinary, and of the route, being tremendous and taking a danger doesn't suggest the whole lot will flip out the way we'd have was hoping. College students who examine their mistakes can still cognizant of the high-quality facet of factors. Preserve a high-quality outlook, and respect the valuable instructions and understanding and college students can proportion the stories of the ones as well.

Combine effective affirmations for children and proprioceptive input with the high-quality course. Children can bounce alongside the direction or do wall push-u.s.at the same time as they examine phrases of encouragement. College students can benefit from proprioceptive enter to assist get their bodies prepared to learn. The advantageous course highlights the importance of a nice mindset for college students. The use of the power of nice wondering with each day affirmations and bodily activity can assist students to get their brains and our bodies ready to tackle the college day.

Studying methods

In comparison to the psychodynamic techniques of Freud and the neo-Freudians, which relate personality to inner (and hidden) procedures, the studying techniques recognition most effective on observable behavior. This illustrates one large advantage of gaining knowledge of procedures to persona over psychodynamics: due to the fact getting to know approaches involve observable, measurable phenomena, they can be scientifically examined.

• The Behavioral perspective

Behaviorists do not agree with organic determinism: They

do no longer see personality developments as inborn. Rather, they view persona as notably fashioned via the reinforcements and consequences outdoor of the organism. In different phrases, people behave regularly based on the previous studies. B. F. Skinner, a strict behaviorist, believed that surroundings changed into entirely accountable for all conduct, which includes the enduring, constant behavior styles studied by way of character theorists.

As you can remember out of your study on the psychology of getting to know, Skinner proposed that we exhibit consistent conduct patterns due to the fact we have developed certain response tendencies. In different words, we learn to behave mainly ways. We increase the behaviors that result in fantastic effects, and we decrease the behaviors that lead to terrible consequences. Skinner disagreed with Freud's concept that persona is constant in youth. He argued that character develops over our entire lifestyles, not simplest inside the first few years. Our responses can trade as we stumble upon new conditions; consequently, we will assume more variability over time in persona than Freud might expect. For instance, keep in mind a young female, Greta, a chance taker. She drives speedily and participates in risky sports activities which include grasp gliding and kiteboarding. But after she receives married and has kids, the device of reinforcements and punishments in her environment modifications. Rushing and excessive sports activities are not strengthened, so she does not engage in one's behaviors. In truth, Greta now describes herself as a cautious character.

- The Social-Cognitive angle

Albert Bandura agreed with Skinner that persona develops through getting to know. He disagreed, however, with Skinner's strict behaviorist method to character improvement, due to the fact he felt that questioning and reasoning are critical components of getting to know. He presented a social-cognitive principle of character that emphasizes each gaining knowledge of and cognition as sources of person differences in personality. In social-cognitive theory, the concepts of reciprocal determinism, observational studying, and self-efficacy all play a component in personality improvement.

- Reciprocal Determinism

In comparison to Skinner's idea that the surroundings by myself determine behavior, Bandura (1990) proposed with the concept of reciprocal determinism, wherein cognitive approaches, behavior, and context all have interaction, each aspect influencing and being inspired through the others simultaneously (Cognitive methods consult with all traits previously discovered, together with beliefs, expectancies, and character characteristics. Behavior refers to something that we do that can be rewarded or punished. Sooner or later, the context in which the behavior happens refers to the environment or situation, which incorporates worthwhile/punishing stimuli.

Don't forget, as an instance, which you're at a pageant and one of the sights is bungee jumping from a bridge. Do you do it? In this situation, the conduct is bungee leaping. Cognitive elements that could influence this behavior encompass your beliefs and values, and your past reviews with comparable behaviors. In the end, context refers back to the reward structure for the behavior. Consistent with reciprocal determinism, all of those factors are in play.

Observational getting to know

Bandura's key contribution to learning concept become the concept that lots gaining knowledge of is vicarious. We examine through looking at a person else's behavior and its results, which Bandura known as observational gaining knowledge of. He felt that this form of mastering also performs a component inside the improvement of our personality. Simply as we learn personal behaviors, we research new behavior styles when we see them achieved via different human beings or models. Drawing at the behaviorists' ideas approximately reinforcement, Bandura counseled that whether or not we choose to imitate a version's behavior relies upon whether or not we see the model bolstered or punished. Through observational gaining knowledge, we come to learn what behaviors are suitable and rewarded in our tradition, and we also learn to inhibit deviant or socially unacceptable behaviors through seeing what behaviors are punished. We can see the principles of reciprocal determinism at work in observational studying. As an instance, non-public factors determine which behaviors inside the surroundings a person chooses to imitate, and those environmental activities, in turn, are processed cognitively according to different private elements.

Self-Efficacy

Bandura (1977, 1995) has studied several cognitive and personal elements that affect learning and persona development, and maximum recently has targeted the concept of self-efficacy. Self-efficacy is our degree of confidence in our personal competencies, advanced through our social stories. Self-efficacy influences how we approach challenges and attain dreams. In observational gaining knowledge of, self-efficacy is a cognitive factor that affects which behaviors we choose to imitate in addition to our achievement in performing those behaviors.

People who've excessive self-efficacy believe that their goals are inside reach, have a high-quality view of demanding situations seeing them as responsibilities to be mastered, develop a deep hobby in and sturdy dedication to the sports wherein they are concerned, and quickly get over setbacks. Conversely, people with low self-efficacy avoid hard obligations due to the fact they doubt their potential to be successful, generally tend to attention to failure and negative effects, and lose self-assurance of their abilities if they enjoy setbacks. Emotions of self-efficacy may be precise to positive situations. As an instance, a student may feel assured in her potential in English elegance however much less so in math magnificence.

Julian Rotter and Locus manipulating

Julian Rotter (1966) proposed the concept of locus of manipulating, any other cognitive aspect that impacts studying and personality development. Awesome from self-efficacy, which entails our belief in our personal skills, locus of manipulating refers to our beliefs approximately the power we have over our lives. Human beings possess both an inner and an external locus of control. Those of us with an inner locus of control ("internals") generally tend to agree that the maximum of our effects is the direct result of our efforts. those of us with an external locus of control ("externals") tend to accept as true that our consequences are outdoor of our manage. Externals see their lives as being controlled with the aid of different humans, success, or hazard. For instance, say you didn't spend tons of time analyzing your psychology check and went out to dinner with friends alternatively. when you obtain your test score, you notice that you earned a D. if you possess an internal locus of manipulation, you would most possibly admit which you failed due to the fact you didn't spend enough time studying and decide to study greater for the following take a look at. On the other hand, in case you possess an external locus of manage, you may finish that the test turned into too tough and not trouble reading for the next take a look at, because you parent you will fail it anyway. Researchers have determined that human beings with an inner locus of management carry out better academically, attain greater of their careers, are more independent, are more healthy, are higher able to cope, and are much less depressed than humans who have an external locus of manage.

Humanistic processes

As the "one-third pressure" in psychology, humanism is touted as a reaction both to the pessimistic determinism of psychoanalysis, with its emphasis on psychological disturbance, and to the behaviorists' view of people passively reacting to the surroundings, which has been criticized as making human beings out to be character-less robots. It does now not advocate that psychoanalytic, behaviorist, and other factors of view are wrong but argues that those perspectives do now not apprehend the intensity and which means of human experience, and fail to recognize the innate capability for self-directed alternate and reworking non-public studies. This angle focuses on how healthful human beings broaden. One pioneering humanist, Abraham Maslow, studied folks that he considered being wholesome, creative, and effective, inclusive of Albert Einstein, Eleanor Roosevelt, Thomas Jefferson, Abraham Lincoln, and others. He observed that such human beings percentage similar traits, inclusive of being open, innovative, loving, spontaneous, compassionate, involved for others, and accepting of themselves. When you studied motivation, you discovered approximately one of the high-quality-recognized humanistic theories, Maslow's hierarchy of wishes theory, wherein Maslow proposes that people have positive wishes in the commonplace and that those desires have to be met in a sure order. The best need is the need for self-actualization, which is the fulfillment of our fullest capability.

Another humanistic theorist became Carl Rogers. Certainly one of Rogers's main ideas about persona regards self-idea, our thoughts and emotions approximately ourselves. How might you respond to the question, "Who am I?" Your answer can show the way you see yourself. If your reaction is basically positive, then you definitely have a tendency to be ok with whom you are, and also you see the arena as a safe and tremendous location. If your reaction is especially negative, then you could feel sad about who you're. Rogers similarly divided the self into categories: the right self and the real self. The correct self is the person who you would really like to be; the real self is the person you certainly are. Rogers centered on the concept that we want to attain consistency between those selves. We revel in congruence while our thoughts approximately our real self and perfect self are very similar—in different phrases, whilst our self-ideal is accurate.

High congruence ends in a more feel of self-worth and a healthy full, effective lifestyle. Parents can assist their youngsters to obtain this by giving them unconditional positive regard, or unconditional love. As men and women are customary and prized, they tend to develop a greater being concerned attitude in the direction of themselves. Human beings rose in surroundings of unconditional fine regard, wherein no preconceived situations of well worth are a gift, have the possibility to absolutely actualize. While human beings are raised in surroundings of conditional advantageous regard, wherein well worth and love are handiest given beneath positive situations, they have to healthy or reap the one's conditions if you want to receive the love or tremendous regard they yearn for. Their best self is thereby decided by others primarily based on those situations, and they're compelled to develop outside of their own authentic actualizing tendency; this contributes to incongruence and an extra gap between the real self and the suitable self. Both Rogers's and Maslow's theories cognizance of individual choices and do no longer agree that biology is deterministic.

Unconditional superb regard

Within the development of the self-concept, Rogers improved the significance of unconditional effective regard or unconditional love. Character development and the Self-idea: Rogers primarily based his theories of persona improvement on humanistic psychology and theories of subjective experience. He believed that everyone exists in a constantly changing world of experiences that they're in the middle of. A person reacts to adjustments of their exceptional subject, which includes outside gadgets and people as well as inner mind and feelings. Rogers believed that everyone's behavior is stimulated through self-actualizing inclinations, which pressure a person to achieve at their highest degree. due to their interactions with the environment and others, a man or woman paperwork a structure of the self or self-idea—an organized, fluid, conceptual pattern of concepts and values associated with the self. If a person has a tremendous self-idea, they tend to be ok with which they may be and frequently see the arena as a secure and high-quality place. If they have a bad self-concept, they'll sense unhappy with who they may be.

Chapter Eight

Academic Discourse

Instructional discourse, additionally known as the concept of how students speak discoveries and establish that reference to their universal getting to know, is a precious thing to remember in coaching. The conversation is important for any scholar to be successful, and academic discourse locations emphasis on the right conversation to enable progress in classwork and projects. Educational discourse is likewise encompassing the concept of discussion, from the language utilized by college students to the facilitation of conversation within the schoolroom, precise educational discourse is a vital skill for students. Encouraging better tiers of communique, in anything from complete elegance discussions to look-to-peer verbal exchange, can help students to enhance their trouble-based studying.

Traits of instructional discourse

Discourse can include something from paying attention to debating, presentations to meta-cognition, and even writing to critique. Teaching your students to communicate and interact using instructional vocabulary is at the heart of educational discourse. Asking the proper questions is considered one of the correct locations to start. For most of the people of students, the concept of academic discourse isn't always one that comes naturally. Instead, it needs to be modeled through educators, and both taught and identified by way of college students and instructors. Strategic practice is important to offer students insight into what instructional discourse is, in addition to what it feels and looks as if. Integrating this ability constructing can enrich lecture room verbal exchange, and inspire deeper retention and learning. This manner gives insight into how this skill may be described and carried out in a math study room putting:

• The expectation is set that students should present issues, after which explain how they reached a solution.

• The significance of the right vocabulary and phrase exercise is said, ensuring students have a distinction among distinctive phrases – inclusive of an equation and an expression.

• Using writing in the math study room is elevated, with teachers requiring students to put in writing no longer best their answer, but the process of accomplishing that answer. This permits them to manner fabric and practices applicable vocabulary.

Complex problem fixing

With a hassle-based total curriculum of gaining knowledge, college students are brought to increasingly complex problems to solve. This technique of education encourages more active verbal exchange between students in ways that man or woman duties or homework does no longer. A study room with remarkable academic discourse is an extra meaningful one, beyond certainly soaking up the problem count you are given. An example unit will be 'how could a store maximize the income they make', with students working in organizations to remedy the query-based totally on take a look at and trouble fixing as a unit. In this example, college students may want to utilize their records to create a quadratic equation to determine income based on their collaborative work. This sort of has to look should be completed along with mastering quadratics, to offer greater potential for the issue and higher levels of hassle solving.

- Processing what every axis means or represents
- Establishing the relevance of income, price, and earnings in this particular context
- Identifying and connecting the want for smash-even factors plus the vertex

With this sort of complex hassle fixing, academic discourse can soon become second nature, allowing college students to expand further understanding of each subject count and the blessings of running with the better verbal exchange. Within the case of the above PBL task, college students require the support of each other to establish a robust notion process, making educational discourse a natural end. The key isn't in constantly getting the right answer; it's in using the thought procedure efficaciously to reach an extra knowledgeable end.

Instructional discourse network

As such, responsibilities that require collaborative problem-fixing offer enough ways to assess and test a student's use of interactivity and vocabulary. This trouble solving additionally offers college students a way to self-assess their development and information of a challenge or difficulty. Starting with vocabulary games or maybe having students re-evaluate formerly written text can be tremendous methods to assist students system these new competencies and strategies. Once a unit is finished in the schoolroom that requires group communication, academic discourse will become that tons easier. Quickly, college students will flow from being insular of their getting to know to set up better peer verbal exchange, and should for lively studying. With practice and consistency, college students can deepen their learning and knowledge way to these essential skills.

Academic language discourse

Academic discourse is greater than just a tool for the education gadget; it's additionally a technique of problem-solving that can be carried beyond the walls of a study room. Some of the lengthy-time period advantages of employing these strategies include:

• Extended communique among college students, allowing for higher mastering experiences

• Progressed problem-fixing skills each in huge agencies and smaller initiatives

• Better conversation competencies as a whole, with both peers and educators

• Deeper understanding of the concerned matter, and the relevance it carries when fixing troubles

• Enhanced vocabulary each in verbal exchange and in writing conclusions and evaluation

Academic Discourse

To recognize the concept of instructional discourse one, ought to recognize what the means academic discourse is. Discourse is a common phrase. The word of discourse can be interchanged with discussion or communique in normal speech or writing (Washington nation Libraries). Discourse is a proper dialogue of a topic with the usage of speech or writing the usage of the communication of phrases. Discourse is a written or spoken approach to a topic that is treated or discussed at a period (Washington country Libraries). The discourse among people wishes to have a number of the same traits. As an instance, they want to speak the same language (Elbow). But extra is going into the discourse between those people than just the identical language. The discourse has shared assumptions and the same cultural values even shared slang. Agencies of people that share those traits are referred to as discourse groups. Doctors, scientists, regulation officials, and mechanics make up their personal unique discourse network. Normally to be usual within the discourse network one could have to communicate inside the lingo of the sure profession. Discourse groups have positive lingo, norms, and commonplace understanding whilst communicating within the network. This especially goes for writing.

If two articles are as compared, one from the journal of Soil and Water Conservation and a piece of writing from the international journal of Police technological know-how and management, the differences can be without difficulty depicted. The discourse of a magazine additionally method how it's miles set up. In the journal of Soil and Water Conservation, the articles are set up in a certain way. In the pinnacle, the left-hand nook of the article is wherein the sort of article is shown. In the case of the object "Scaling from subject to area for wind erosion prediction the use of Wind Erosion Prediction device and geographical information structures" the type of article is called "implemented studies". Proper beneath this is the name of the article in formidable black print that may be larger font than the rest of the item. Beneath the identifying is the listing of the authors, which is normally double, spaced from the title of the thing. Another space is the "abstract". The "summary" is a quick precis paragraph of the item; after the "summary" are the "key phrases" of the item. Double spaced from the "key terms" is the "advent". The advent's first sentence of the object is bolded in black. The rest of the thing is then broken up into "materials and approach", "consequences and discussions" and "precis and conclusions". The "methods and materials" part of the article is just the assessments and materials used within the experiments. There are commonly graphs and tables in the "methods and materials" too. Each of the graphs and maps is labeled, discern one or discern two, it topics the orders wherein they appear. Everyone also has a short description of what the figure represents. The "result and dialogue" part of the article just explains the effects of the experiments done and discusses how the outcomes came about. The "effects and discussions" additionally have figures that show the consequences of the experiments and check. The "summary and conclusions" is the how and why bit of the paper. In this part of the item, they explain why some of the consequences came out the manner they did, and then it makes conclusions from all of the statistics of the "outcomes" part of the object. The thing constantly has figures that display and lower back up the belief offered. As soon as the "precis and conclusions" is finished the article has "acknowledgments". The "acknowledgments" give rewards to the groups and people who funded the research supplied inside the article. After the "acknowledgments" are the "references" in which the authors provide different authors and people reputation for the thoughts and records they used for the thing.

Inside the journal of Police technology and management set their article up a little one of a kind than that of the natural sources journal. In the pinnacle left corner of the primary page, the thing offers the journal's name and the extent of it. In the middle, the "identify" that's bolded in black and the font is greater too. Right under the "identify" are the author's names addresses and email addresses. Also, there is the date wherein the object changed into received, edited, and established within the magazine. Beneath this data are the "key phrases" of the object. After the "keywords" is information on each of the authors. These statistics include the writer's schooling, profession, function, and achievements. They have these records for each creator. After all of the facts approximately the author is the "abstract" which is a one-paragraph summary of the item. In this journal, the "summary is italicized. After the "abstract is the "advent" to the item. The relaxation of the paper is broken up into subtopics that are bolded in black and is in large font so it is straightforward to follow. The thing does have statistics that are provided in graphs and tables and each one is categorized in figures. Underneath the labels is the outline of what each graph is supplying. On the give up of the item is the "end" in which the authors make conclusions from the records they presented in the article. The "references" is after the "conclusion". The "references" a part of the item is where the authors deliver reputation to the human beings from whom they took thoughts and information.

The statistics given approximately the two special magazine articles indicate that each of those discourse groups has one-of-a-kind ways in which they convey records to their community. Each of those discourses even cites their references distinct. Now not everybody can study a piece of writing out of the magazine of Soil and Water Conservation and apprehend all this is said. This is because the magazine within the natural resource uses vocabulary and lingo that isn't usually used or seen. Someone that might recognize these articles of the herbal assets will both be in this field and have a little know-how of this discourse. Even if one is aware of the definition of positive phrases in the article, the words should have a different meaning wherein they're generally described using. The item in the journal of Police technology and management is plenty less difficult to study and follow. The item flows properly, type of like a tale or rationalization. This newsletter does no longer split up into parts that have tests and materials. These articles in this magazine commonly use common vocabulary that everybody can read and won't need to have tons of know-how of the profession. This journal makes use of APA style to quote assets while the journal of Soil and Water Conservation makes use of the style of CBE. Discourse within the two professions uses distinctive lingo and jargon in their discussions of a subject. That is the same for any two specific discourse groups. Discourse is a style of writing and conversation of a formal difficulty (Washington nation Libraries).

Instructional discourse refers to the ways of thinking and the use of language which exist inside the academy. Its importance, in huge element, lies within the reality that complicated social activities like instructing students, demonstrating studying, disseminating thoughts, and building information, depend upon language to accomplish. Textbooks, essays, convention displays, dissertations, lectures, and research articles are relevant to the academic enterprise and are the very stuff of education and understanding introduction.

However instructional discourse does more than permit universities to get on with the business of coaching and research. It simultaneously constructs the social roles and relationships which create lecturers and students and which sustain the colleges, the disciplines, and the advent of understanding itself. individuals use language to write down, frame problems and understand issues in methods unique to particular social organizations, and in doing these items they form social realities, private identities, and professional establishments. Discourse is at the coronary heart of the educational business enterprise; it is the way that individuals collaborate and compete with others, create know-how, teach neophytes, expose learning, and outline academic allegiances. The academy cannot be separated from its discourses and couldn't exist without them. No discovery, perception, invention, or information has any importance until it's made to be had to others and no college or person will get hold of credit score for it till it has seen the light of day via e-book.

To one degree then, the take a look at academic discourse is interesting for what it can tell us approximately the accomplishment of instructional life. However, past the college, the languages of the academy have quietly begun to insert themselves into each cranny of our lives, colonizing the discourses of technocracy, bureaucracy, leisure, and advertising. Educational discourses have reshaped our whole international view, turning into the dominant mode for deciphering truth and our very own life. We find traces of it now not just in popular technology periodicals however within the Sunday broadsheets and the television documentary, it's the language of the pharmaceutical bottle and the toothpaste advertisement, the psychotherapist, and the recycling leaflet. It's the service of expertise and status - the badge of folks who possess the expertise and of people who want to. The language of science has come to be the language of literacy'. There are consequently suitable reasons for taking educational discourse critically, and in this bankruptcy, I will are trying to find to expose why academic discourse is essential, something of what is thought approximately it, and how it is studied, carrying out with a sample observe which illustrates those problems.

Why is academic discourse important?

The current interest in academic discourse, and mainly educational writing in English, is largely the result of three fundamental trends during the last twenty years: modifications in higher schooling which have ended in extra hobby given to the significance of writing; the boom of English because the global language of research and scholarship; and the emergence of theoretical views which recognize the centrality of academic discourses within the creation of information.

First, many countries in Europe, Asia, and Australasia have witnessed a massive expansion of higher training as a result of more social inclusion guidelines. This growth has been observed via increases in complete charge paying worldwide college students to compensate for cuts in government help and using the speedy rise in refugee populations around the world with a consequent growth in international migration. Collectively these factors have created a student body that's a long way extra culturally, socially, and linguistically heterogeneous than ever before. Delivered to that is the fact that students now take a broader and greater eclectic blend of topics. The 'academicization' of exercise-based totally disciplines such as nursing, social work, and advertising and the growth of modular and inter-disciplinary tiers approach that students must analyze swiftly to negotiate a complicated web of disciplinary particular textual content-types, evaluation tasks, and presentational modes (each face-to-face and online) so that it will graduate.

So at the same time as writing remains the way wherein college students each consolidate and displays the know-how of their topics and are socialized into educational practices, students, which includes native English speakers, ought to take on new roles and engage with knowledge in new approaches after they enter college. A crucial result of these adjustments is that newcomers deliver different identities, understandings, and behavior of which means-making to a greater various variety of subjects, so that tutors cannot expect their college students will possess the understandings and learning studies to equip them with the literacy abilities historically required in university publications. As a result, greater emphasis is now placed on academic literacy and on EAP programs to assist college students to meet the needs of their guides.

Instructional discourses had been considerably studied to tell this pedagogic agenda.

A second motive for this developing interest in educational discourse has been the power it wields inside the careers of individual teachers. Publishing is the principal way using which academics establish their claims for competence and climb the professional ladder. Furthermore, as pressures on lecturers to publish increase, so does the demand that this ought to be finished in English. Studies show that academics all around the globe are increasingly much less in all likelihood to post in their personal languages and to locate their English language guides referred to more regularly. There had been over 1.1 million peer-reviewed research articles published globally in English in 2005 and this quantity has been increasing by using four percent yearly. With publishers encouraging libraries to subscribe to online variations of journals, the effect of English becomes self-perpetuating because it's far in those journals in which authors could be maximumly visible on the arena stage and acquire the most credit. This has intended that the number of non-native English speaking lecturers publishing in English language journals now exceed papers authored via native English speakers and driving demand for writing for e-book courses. In this enterprise, the examining of academic discourse has to turn out to be relevant to pedagogy.

A third most important incentive for analyzing educational discourse comes from a very one-of-a-kind course: the questioning of a positivist, empirical view of clinical expertise. In latest years the view of academic discourse as an objective, impartial demonstration of absolute fact has been challenged by way of the sociology of clinical knowledge. Basically, this attitude argues that medical evidence does no longer lay within the software of unbiased methodologies but in academic arguments. Observations are as fallible as the theories they presuppose, and so texts cannot be seen as accurate representations of 'what the arena is absolutely like' due to the fact this illustration is continually filtered through acts of selection and foregrounding. In different phrases, there's always more than one viable interpretation of information, and those competing motives shift interest from the laboratory or clipboard to the methods that teachers argue their claims. We need to search for proof in the textual practices for producing settlement. on the coronary heart of instructional persuasion, then, is writers' tries to anticipate and head off possible negative reactions to their claims, and to try this they use the discourses in their disciplines.

Interest in educational discourse has consequently emerged as a part of tries to reveal the specific rhetorical practices of instructional persuasion. Analysts are seeking to find out how human beings use discourse to get their thoughts typical and at the same time how this works to assemble knowledge and sustain alternate disciplinary groups. This is key trouble of instructional discourse analysis and the look at human interplay more generally, as Stubbs (1996: 21) observes: The primary intellectual puzzle in the social sciences is the relation among the micro and the macro. How is it that habitual normal behavior, from second to moment, can create and keep social institutions over long durations of time?

On this organization discourse analysis, in particular text-based forms of style evaluation, has become installed as the maximum extensively used and effective method.

How is instructional discourse studied?

Discourse analysis comprises a huge collection of strategies for studying language in action, looking at texts about the social contexts wherein they're used. Because language is an irreducible part of social life, this huge definition has been interpreted in numerous ways across the social sciences. In instructional contexts, but, it has tended to be a method that specializes in concrete texts rather than institutional social practices. Particularly, it has in large part taken the form of that to specialize in precise academic genres along with the research article, conference presentation, and student essay. Genre analysis can be visible as a greater unique form of discourse analysis that focuses on any detail of recurrent language use, along with grammar and lexis, which applies to the analyst's pursuits. As a result, genre analysis sees texts as representative of wider rhetorical practices and so has the capability to provide descriptions and reasons for each text and the groups that use them.

Genres are recurrent makes use of extra-or-less conventionalized forms through which individuals expand relationships, set up communities, and get things finished the usage of language. Genres can as a consequence be visible as a form of tacit contract among writers and readers, which have an impact on the behavior of textual content manufacturers and the expectations of receivers. Through focusing on mapping typicality, style analysis for that reason seeks to show what is standard in collections of texts and so helps to reveal underlying ideologies and discourses and the alternatives of disciplinary communities. those strategies are encouraged by using Halliday's (1994) view of language as a machine of selections that hyperlink texts to specific contexts through styles of lexico-grammatical and rhetorical functions and by using Swales' (1990) commentary that these recurrent alternatives are carefully associated with the work of unique discourse communities whose individuals share extensive social purposes.

One of the most efficient applications of discourse analysis to academic texts has been to explore the lexico-grammatical regularities of unique genres to pick out their structural identification. Studying this type of patterning has yielded useful facts about the approaches texts are built and how we recognize coherent patterning of textual content elements. Some of these studies have accompanied the pass evaluation work pioneered with the aid of Swales (1990) which seeks to discover the ranges of specific institutional genres and the constraints on usual move sequences. Moves are the rhetorical steps which writers or audio system robotically use to develop their social functions, and recent work on academic genres has produced descriptions of dissertation acknowledgments and the methods sections in studies articles.

Whilst analyzing schematic structures has proved a useful manner of looking at texts, analysts are an increasing number of aware the risks of oversimplifying with the aid of assuming blocks of texts to be mono-practical and ignoring writers' complicated purposes and "non-public intentions". There may be additionally the problem of validating analyses to make certain they are no longer simply products of the analyst's intuitions. Transitions from one circulate to any other are continually motivated out of doors the text as writers reply to their social context, however, analysts have now not always been capable of become aware of the ways those shifts are explicitly signaled via lexico-grammatical patterning. consequently, attention has grown to become too specific capabilities of specific genres, both grammatical, which includes condition adverbials in scholarly shows, purposeful, like hedging in studies articles, or rhetorical, which includes assessment in book reviews. Corpora are increasingly used to pick out frequent choices in extraordinary modes and genres, with recent studies exploring the common four-phrase collocations, or lexical bundles, which are traditional in undergraduate textbooks and scholar dissertations.

Whilst text evaluation is a vital part of discourse analysis, discourse evaluation is not merely the linguistic evaluation of texts. In educational contexts, the interpretive and qualitative look at each text and user has begun to grow in the latest years to establish the methods that texts are firmly embedded inside the cultures and activities wherein their customers take part. One example is earlier's (1998) study of the contexts and approaches of graduate student writing at a US college. Drawing on transcripts of seminar discussions, student texts, observations of institutional contexts, train feedback, and interviews with college students and tutors, prior gives an in-intensity account of the ways students in 4 fields negotiated their writing responsibilities and so became socialized into their disciplinary groups. another examination suggests how advice from supervisors, a magazine editor, and reviewers helped guide a Chinese doctoral pupil of physics thru six drafts and several resubmissions earlier than her paper were finally time-honored for the booklet.

Ethnographic-oriented research has additionally explored the literate cultures of academics themselves. Possibly the first-rate acknowledged of those is Swales' (1998) 'textography' of his building at the college of Michigan. Swales makes more use of analyses of texts and systems of texts in his approach than lots ethnography, combining discourse analyses with huge observations and interviews. Collectively these techniques provide a richly distinct image of the professional lives, commitments, and tasks of people in three various instructional cultures working within the construction: the laptop center, the Herbarium, and the thUniversityty English Language Centre. The interaction of various sorts of records permits us to see how a couple of influences of academic practices, friends, mentors, and personal reviews all contribute to their texts and experiences as educational writers.

Subsequently, studies conducted from an important angle have targeted how social relations, identification, information, and power are constructed through written and spoken texts in disciplines, schools, and classrooms. outstanding using a brazenly political timetable, CDA has tried to expose that the discourses of the academy are not a transparent or impartial way for describing the sector however works to assemble alter and control understanding, social relations, and establishments. particular literacy practices own authority because they constitute the currently dominant ideological methods of depicting relationships and realities and those legal methods of seeing the arena exercising control of lecturers and college students alike. Lillis (2001), as an example, show how this may create tensions for college kids in coping with university literacy demands, whilst other research shows comparable worries among Non-local English students.

What can we recognize about instructional discourse?

together those distinctive methods goal at taking pictures thicker descriptions of language use in the academy, producing a wealthy vein of study's findings which maintains to inform each teaching and our understanding of the practices of disciplinary knowledge-making. The size of this research is hard to summarize, but we can discover the four most important findings:

• That educational genres are persuasive and systematically established to secure readers' settlement;

• That these ways of producing settlement constitute disciplinary particular rhetorical possibilities;

• That language organizations have specific methods of expressing thoughts and structuring arguments;

• That educational persuasion includes interpersonal negotiations as much as convincing ideas.

Academic texts are established for persuasive impact

All educational texts are designed to steer readers of something: of the knowledge declare on the heart of a research article or dissertation; of an assessment of others' work in a book overview, or one's understanding and intellectual autonomy in an undergraduate essay. To perform those numerous purposes, writers tend to draw at an equal repertoire of linguistic resources for every style time and again. That is, in part, because writing is an exercise primarily based on expectations. The technique of writing includes developing a text that the author assumes the reader will apprehend and count on and the process of analyzing entails drawing on assumptions about what the author is trying to do. Hoey (2001) says that that is like dancers following every other's steps, each assembling feel from a textual content with the aid of awaiting what the alternative is probably to do using making connections to prior texts. At the same time as writing, like dancing, allows for creativity and the surprising, established styles shape the idea of any versions.

This schema of earlier expertise received thru formal learning and repeated studies with texts, permits writers and audio system to specific themselves appropriately and correctly, drawing on conventions for organizing messages so that their readers can recognize their cause and follows their thoughts. The studies article, as an instance, is a genre that restructures the strategies of notion and the studies it describes to set up a discourse for medical fact-creation. The language will become a shape of generation on this incredibly subtle genre because it attempts to present interpretations and role individuals mainly ways as a means of establishing understanding.

Several spoken and written educational genres have been studied in current years. Those consist of scholarly dissertations, convention shows, and supply proposals. We can see the huge versions of those functions throughout the two genres. The more use of hedging underlines the want for caution and opens up arguments in the studies papers in comparison with the legal certainties of the textbook, even as the elimination of citation in textbooks suggests how statements are presented as facts rather than claims grounded inside the literature. The more use of self-mention in articles factors to the private stake that writers spend money on their arguments and their preference to gain credit score for claims. The better frequency of transitions, which can be conjunctions and other linking alerts, within the textbooks is a result of the truth that writers need to make connections some distance greater specific for readers with much less subject matter understanding.

Academic represent discipline-unique modes of argument texts

Another finding of studies is that a hit educational writing depends on the person writer's control of the epistemic conventions of a field, what counts as suitable proof and argument, and that this differs throughout fields. Studies on language variants across the disciplines are now one of the more fruitful traces of research and one of the dominant paradigms in EAP.

The idea of the area is rather nebulous but captures how people use and respond to language as participants of social groups. Challenged by way of postmodernism, interdisciplinary studies, and the emergence of modular ranges, the belief of area is regularly wondered, but even as limitations are in no way stable nor objects of study immutable, the subject is a belief with outstanding endurance. Their distinctiveness, however, may be knowledgeable via examination of rhetorical practices.

That is because successful instructional writing relies upon writers' projections of a shared expert context as they searching for to embed their writing in a specific social world which they mirror and conjure up through approved discourses.

Essentially, we can see disciplines as the language they use of groups, and this facilitates us to be part of writers, texts, and readers collectively. Communities provide the context inside which we learn how to communicate and to interpret each other's communication, steadily obtaining the specialized discourse skills to participate as participants. So we can see disciplines as particular recognized and acquainted methods of doing things – especially of the usage of language to engage with others. Audio system and writers accordingly make language choices to benefit assist, express collegiality and solve problems in methods which fit the network's assumptions, strategies, and information. Each difficult subject constitutes a manner of making feel of human revel in that has evolved over generations and each is dependent on its very own precise practices: its instrumental techniques, its criteria for judging relevance and validity, and its conventions of applicable styles of argument. In a word each has advanced its very own modes of discourse. So disciplines shape research inside wider frameworks of beliefs and provide the conventions and expectations that make texts meaningful.

Inside the sciences, new know-how is established thru experimental evidence. Science writing reinforces this via highlighting an opening in knowledge, offering speculation associated with this hole, and then reporting experimental findings to assist this. The humanities, then again, depending upon case studies and narratives at the same time as claims are prevalent on electricity of argument. The social sciences fall among these poles due to the fact in making use of clinical methods to much less predictable human records they should deliver extra attention to specific interpretation. In different words, instructional discourse allows providing identification to an area, and analyses of texts assist reveal the distinct approaches disciplines have of asking questions, addressing literature, criticizing ideas, and supplying arguments. Research has observed extensive rhetorical variation throughout a variety of capabilities in genres which includes medical letters, writing assignments, and Ph.D. dissertations.

One of the most placing differences in how language differs throughout fields is the usage of hedges which include possible, would possibly, probable, and so forth. This feature withholds the entire commitment to a proposition, implying that a declaration is based on viable reasoning in place of positive knowledge. They suggest the diploma of self-belief the writer thinks it might be clever to provide a claim even as starting a discursive area for readers to dispute interpretations. Because they represent the author's direct involvement in textual content, something that scientists usually try to keep away from, they are two times as common in humanities and social technology papers as in tough sciences. One purpose for this is there may be much less management of variables, extra variety of study consequences, and fewer clean bases for accepting claims than inside the sciences. Writers can't record studies with the equal confidence of shared assumptions so papers rely ways more on spotting alternative voices. Arguments ought to be expressed more carefully by using more hedges. Inside the hard sciences, positivist epistemologies suggest that the authority of the man or woman is subordinated to the authority of the text, and facts are supposed to 'speak for themselves. Writers therefore often hide their interpretative activities in the back of linguistic objectivity. They downplay their personal function to indicate that outcomes will be equal to whoever conducted the research. The less frequent use of hedges is one way of conducting this.

Unique cultures have one-of-a-kind language schemata

Educational discourse evaluation has additionally pointed to cultural specificity in rhetorical alternatives. Even though an arguable time period, one version of subculture regards it as a traditionally transmitted and systematic community of meanings that permit us to recognize, broaden and speak our expertise and ideals approximately the sector. Culture is visible as inextricably bound up with language, so that cultural elements have the potential to influence perception, language, gaining knowledge of, and conversation. Even though it is far from conclusive, discourse analytic studies show that the schemata of L2 and L1 writers range in their desired ways of organizing thoughts which could influence academic writing. Those conclusions were supported by way of several studies into distinct genres over the last decade.

A lot of this work has targeted scholarly genres and has diagnosed a selection of different functions in first and second language writing in English, in particular, the ways writers include fabric into their writing, how they orientate to readers via attention-getting devices, and estimates of reader expertise, and differences inside the use of overt linguistic capabilities (consisting of much less subordination, greater conjunction, less passivation, fewer free modifiers, less noun-amendment, much less precise words, less lexical range, predictable version, and a less complicated fashion). Critics factor out, but, that due to the fact contrastive rhetoric begins from an assumption of difference, it has "tended to study L2 writing, especially as a hassle of the negative switch of L1 rhetorical styles to L2 writing". This no longer best sees L2 writing as a deficit, however, runs the risk of ignoring the wealthy and complex histories of such students' literacies and what they bring to the L2 study room.

Similarly significantly, tons of the contrastive rhetoric studies into discourse assume an 'obtained view of culture' which unproblematically identifies cultures with country-wide entities and emphasizes predictable consensuality within cultures and differences throughout them. However, it's far truthful to mention that, compared with many languages; instructional writing in English tends to:

• Be extra explicit approximately its structure and functions with consistent previewing and reviewing

• Appoint greater, and extra recent, citations

• Be much less tolerant of digressions

• Be extra cautious in making claims, with great use of mitigation and hedging

• Use greater sentence connectors to expose explicitly how elements of the text hyperlink collectively.

At the same time as we can't truly predict the methods

people are probably to jot down on the premise of assumed cultural trends, discourse studies have shown that students' first language and earlier studying come to steer approaches of organizing thoughts and structuring arguments while writing in English at university.

Instructional argument entails interpersonal negotiations

Tons latest work has focused on how persuasion in diverse genres isn't always simplest completed through the methods thoughts are supplied, but also using the construction of the suitable authorial self and the negotiation of player relationships. At the same time as once taken into consideration a self-obviously objective and impersonal shape of discourse, academic writing is now broadly considered to be a persuasive endeavor. Academics do not actually produce texts that plausibly represent an external truth, however use language to renowned, assemble and negotiate social relations. Discourse analysis has helped to expose how writers provide a credible representation of themselves and their work with the aid of claiming solidarity with readers, comparing their cloth, and acknowledging alternative perspectives. The interplay in academic writing essentially entails 'positioning', or adopting a factor of view about each of the troubles mentioned inside the text and to others who preserve points of view on one's troubles. In persuading readers in their claims writers need to display competence as disciplinary insiders who're, at the least in part, performed via an author-reader communication that situates each of their research and themselves.

Chapter Nine

Asset-based Instruction

In our international, it is commonplace exercise for human beings to recognize their interest in what's damaged and a way to restorative it. This causes human beings to work in a machine utilizing a deficit model. Even as other businesses might also thrive with the deficit version, schooling is not considered one of them. While school's awareness totally on at-danger behaviors exhibited by way of college students, they tend to work reactively in place of proactivity. Within a college, in which the last purpose ought to be pupils getting to know and increase, this approach is wildly unsuccessful. Rather, schools need to the consciousness of figuring out and building up students' assets to create advantageous improvement. This effective improvement emphasizes strengths over weaknesses, resilience over threats, and assets over deficits. Deficit vs asset; a deficit version makes a specialty of what students can't do. If a pupil is underachieving, people who work from a deficit model trust the failure is because the scholar isn't attempting difficult enough. While running from a deficit angle, the practices and assumptions that emerge tend to cover up the skills of college students and teachers. On the other hand, an asset version, or abundance version, makes a specialty of what a student can do: their strengths, competencies, competencies, hobbies, and competencies.

Schools must inspire all educators to have a look at and venture tacit assumptions. "We can make effective modifications when we smash thru the pervasive effect of the deficit paradigm and apprehend the untapped strengths of college students and teachers". Management we promote an asset version for each college student and workforce. Bearing on multiple academic leadership Constituent Council (ELCC) standards, the asset model suits properly into the framework of a hit leadership.

So as for a whole college to work toward an asset version for student and trainer fulfillment, it should be covered inside the shared vision, challenge, and dreams of the school, which is the context of the primary ELCC standard. An asset model addresses ELCC's trends in key regions. The asset model "promotes the fulfillment of every student via sustaining a faculty culture and academic software conducive to student learning through collaboration, trust, and customized mastering surroundings with high expectancies for college students". When the asset version is utilized thru teacher evaluation, it additionally allows in "developing and supervising the educational and management ability of faculty team of workers". Additionally, when an entire community supports an asset model, there are various opportunities for community-figure school partnerships as stated in ELCC popular. We envision asset models rising from the transformational leadership model shared by using Lunenburg and Ornstein (2012). We trust leaders should passionately proportion this imaginative and prescient to help remodel stakeholders' thinking from a deficit technique to an asset-primarily based method. Encouraging faculty creativity to foster college students' property and work proactively is a first step in moving this paradigm. Asset-centered expectations must be modeled with school and staff through figuring out their assets to determine how they can make contributions to the college and community. Evaluation significance of assets students' issues which are induced by unstable behaviors and selections are known to be related to every different. While one at-threat behavior suggests up, there are usually more than one related at-threat behaviors to observe. However, it seems the training area is focusing too heavily on decreasing dangers, whilst a higher emphasis ought to be positioned on building up pupil strengths.

Through their studies, they have compiled a listing of forty belongings students might also have, categorized into what they call internal and external assets. The external property including aid, empowerment, limitations and expectations, and positive use of time relies on the relationships shaped through adults in their lives. The inner assets, alternatively, are skills that scholars expand to guide themselves. These consist of a commitment to gaining knowledge of, wonderful values, social abilities, and superb identification. thru multiple research of over a million students in grades six to twelve executed using seeking Institute, they have tested repeatedly that the extra assets a pupil possesses, the extra thriving behaviors the student showcase, and the much less likely that scholar will showcase risky behaviors. So why wouldn't faculties need to attend to building up that property to put together college students for a brighter and safer destiny? As Scales (1999) factors out, it's far unrealistic to ignore at-risk behaviors altogether. But, a faculty that focuses maximum of their power on asset development will obviously be operating toward threat discount as nicely.

Asset-constructing communities, not the most effective do students construct positive trends while faculties emphasize asset building, however, this new manner of questioning evidently lets in for high degrees of community-determine-faculty partnerships as well, while faculties shed their deficit model, it will become simpler for the community to end up concerned. Oftentimes, network participants grow to be overwhelmed whilst all they listen are the troubles that teenagers have. Whilst the focus shifts to property, community participants can easily work together to accumulate and nurture positive attributes in kids. This creates what Benson, Leffert, Scales, and Blyth (2012) name wholesome groups. "Healthful communities for youngsters and teens are locations with a shared commitment. They are prominent as relational and intergenerational locations that emphasize support, empowerment, obstacles, and opportunities and a shared commitment to developing internal property".

Further, resilience can be fostered in our youngsters whilst households, groups, and faculties work together to offer possibilities for youngsters to be worried within the community and construct relationships with nice adults in their lives. In fact, scholar time spent in teen programs is one of the most predictive factors to an infant's thriving results. Right children packages are tied tightly with the community and offer college students with getting entry to worrying adults, while also instilling the importance of leadership, supporting others, and retaining suitable fitness. As Woolley and Bowen (2007) point out, "the present studies directly exhibits the importance of supportive and caring adults in the lives of youth at risk and stresses the want to create programs and regulations to promote adults in the domestic, ˇ college, and network to be greater available to young people". ˇ Significance of building belongings in middle colleges consistent with Scales (1999) and his search Institute facts, the common adolescent possesses most effective 18 of the 40 indexed property, and this range tends to lower as the scholars become older. The facts display that the average sixth grader possesses assets and this variety decreases constantly until eleventh grade, with the biggest drops occurring in seventh and eighth grade.

Lamentably, colleges generally tend to provide fewer asset-constructing assets or opportunities for students as they develop via the grades, beginning in middle school. With that information, it isn't surprising that success factors in Center College exceedingly determine a pupil's high faculty achievement and the chance of graduation. "It is at some stage in the middle grades that scholars either launch toward achievement and attainment, or slide off course and placed on a path of frustration, failure, and, in the end, early go out from the simplest relaxed direction to adult success". This could most effortlessly be accomplished by creating greater contact time with fine adults and strengthening the circle of relatives-network-college partnerships. Constructing off of that, Woolley and Bowen (2007) suggest mentoring applications to connect students with the community, faculty sports to create more potent student-teacher bonds, and even a network-extensive reputation of companies to permit dad and mom some time without work to be a gift at college capabilities to create stronger pupil-determine bonds. Even without faculty and community-extensive initiatives, instructors play a huge role in constructing college students' belongings.

In truth, as stated with the aid of Lombardi (2016), "in line with a countrywide middle for schooling statistics' (NCES) look at, teachers' expectancies effect scholar achievement extra than a scholar's own motivation". Lombardi maintains via presenting useful strategies teachers can use in their lecture room to highlight student strengths. These include having excessive expectancies for your college students, convincing them that those expectations are workable, helping them dispose of their fear of failure via encouraging them to fail ahead, placing small and plausible dreams, and celebrating successes when those dreams are met earlier than moving ahead similarly. Customized coaching inside the study room can construct college students' property even further. This may be executed by first identifying each child's jewels (capabilities, abilities, and pastimes) and the usage of these to assist the student to grow from where they may be presently academically, socially, and emotionally. Purpose putting, developing mastering inventories, allow students to teach what they realize well, and celebrating any effective takeaways. crucial Questions even as there's a plentiful quantity of research on how the variety of belongings a pupil has correlated to their thriving consequences, there may be nonetheless greater research to be completed. Future studies must take a look at what effects, if any, teaming in a middle school has on imposing an asset version. We also endorse take a look at the sustained outcomes on college students, if any, in a complete okay-12 asset model. It might be beneficial to look at how the asset version affects student lives beyond the k-12 system.

We promote research in schools that successfully focus their vision around this version in a try and visualize how different faculties can make this transition. Advocacy for greater common tremendous interactions with adults for every scholar- whether or not it be with their instructors, their parents, or network members is another crucial element to encompass in this version. An exam of the studies has shown that youth are in large part influenced by all of the adults of their existence. Scales (1999) sums up the vision of asset targeted colleges by using mentioning, "If we surround younger people with admiration and love, assist them competently discover their abilities, interests, and values, deliver them chances to make a difference in their families, schools, and groups, we're metaphorically letting them jump into our palms". irrespective of how vintage a toddler is, all of them need adults which are willing to mentor them, seize them if they fall, and inspire them to get lower back up and attempt again. This may most effectively be done with an asset version.

An asset-based totally method of training is prime in achieving fairness in classrooms across the country. In recent years, while fairness and access efforts shined a mild on marginalized and underrepresented groups, a few efforts handled schools and communities like they had to be "stored." With an asset-primarily based method, every community is treasured; each network has strengths and potential.

What exactly does it suggest to have an "asset-based approach" to training? Within the most effective terms, an asset-based approach specializes in strengths. It views range in thought, lifestyle, and tendencies as nice assets.

Instructors and students alike are valued for what they carry to the schoolroom in preference to being characterized by using what they may need to work on or lack.

"Asset-primarily based coaching seeks to release students' capacity by using focusing on their skills. Also called strengths-based teaching, this approach contrasts with the more commonplace deficit-primarily based style of coaching which highlights college students' inadequacies."

It's additionally vital that teachers exercise asset-primarily based tactics with their friends and school leaders. New instructors must be supported of their tough work to demonstrate efficacy, which includes coaching that is focused on their strengths to build a foundation for gaining new talents. This runs counter to the dangerous burden put on instructors to fulfill unrealistic boom expectancies and the punitive systems that blame instructors for all that may be incorrect in faculties.

Why does an asset-based totally technique in education matter?

Colleges are an increasing number of diverse, but the teacher force nevertheless lacks massive diversity and does not constitute today's pupil demographics. Lately, an editorial within the New York instances highlighted the records: eighty percent of the public and private simple and excessive school teaching force is white. Conversely, of the 50.7 million public college students, forty-eight percent are white, twenty-eight percent Hispanic, sixteen percent black, five percent Asian, and three percent are two or more races.

Instructor guidance programs need to wrestle with this

stark reality. That's why one of the central values of the NYU Steinhardt trainer Residency is an asset-based totally method to training. It seeks to dispose of deficit questioning and harmful biases that hold lower back students, especially those with disabilities, English language novices, and emergent bilinguals, and students of coloration. Trainer residents are taught to observe variety and differences as attributes to be celebrated as opposed to things to conquer.

"We know that the fine and most organic studying builds on what students already understand," said Diana Turk, Director of trainer education at NYU Steinhardt and certainly one of the colleges who developed the instructor Residency. "To attain college students, we need to realize what they realize – no longer simply what they don't understand. We need to look at them – and have they seen themselves – as capable rookies who can analyze and do something."

Take pupil field for example student subject either reflects the asset-based totally approach or the deficit version. An asset-based method focuses on constructing relationships with and knowledge of students instead of punishing them with detentions, suspensions, and expulsions. Jacqueline Richards, a psychotherapist for children and teens, writes approximately this in the latest Edutopia article: "at the same time as a conventional regulations-and-effects discipline is occasionally powerful in stopping unfavorable behaviors, it can have negative results on the lengthy-time period resilience and connection in the network."

"Believe being a scholar who's seen only thru the lens of his or her deficits: because the pupil who can't sit nonetheless in class or disrupts magnificence with outbursts," endured Professor Turk. "Now, believe how it would experience to be that identical pupil, but rather you're seen as the kid who has more strength than everybody else and consequently can get plenty greater completed, or as the kid who smiles at anybody and is constantly in a great mood. That is how asset-based approaches exchange views within the study room."

Exceptional teachers embody variations inside the study room and make deep connections with their nearby groups. That is why instructor residencies across the United States work to recruit greater human beings from various backgrounds. New facts from the countrywide center for instructor Residencies be aware that extra than 50 percent of citizens were recognized as humans of coloration in 2017.

As new, various people enter the coaching profession, an asset-based totally technique is vital to obtain equity and to present all students the education they deserve. It helps all teachers – regardless of their race, ethnicity, or history – learn to build practices that can be culturally responsive and respectful of college students and their communities.

Not anything will derail a classroom faster than study room management challenges, irrespective of how well planned your lesson is. And even when you have the best intentions in thoughts, focusing too much on scholar misbehavior as a problem that needs to be addressed will handiest boom resistance and frustration on the part of the scholars. So what options are you left with?

Shifting your outlook on lecture room behavior and employing an asset-primarily based view of college students can in reality reduce conduct issues while increasing pupil engagement and excitement approximately what they're learning. This is in assessment to a deficit-primarily based view of college students, which focuses on correcting their inadequacies. In this newsletter, we'll examine six blessings asset-based coaching has on improving schoolroom behavior.

What's asset-based teaching?

When I was in the process of earning my coaching diploma, an educator said, I remember analyzing a line of research that looked at "budget of understanding" in students. This was captivating because it turned into the first article I keep in mind reading that considered the scholars' home existence as wonderful and something that would be integrated into the schoolroom and curriculum.

Asset-based coaching has roots in 'budget of expertise.' This philosophy values the positives and strengths that students convey into the study room. Asset-based totally coaching techniques each pupil as an entire man or woman, consisting of their culture, home lifestyles, previous studies, and know-how, with the attitude that each one of these regions may be introduced into the lecture room environment. Boiled all the way down to the nuts and bolts, asset-primarily based coaching is about focusing on college students' strengths and constructing gaining knowledge of round those strengths and their existing information as opposed to highlighting any deficits or cognitive gaps.

Of direction, there are many motives why students misbehave, and asset-primarily based teaching will now not magically treatment all your classroom management troubles. However, it has the potential to address some of the maximum commonplace reasons why college students misbehave.

Advantages of asset-based gaining knowledge

- It focuses on strengths

It's smooth to merely say that we price the strengths of our students, but is that in reality the case in practice? Asset-based coaching makes this a concrete priority. To find out scholar strengths, you want to truly communicate for your students and examine what they create in the lecture room. This allows you to then shape your training around their strengths.

Optionally, you can also pull in an evaluation that identifies strengths. Those tests come up with each person and lecture room-based totally view of strengths. On a personal degree, this would permit you to higher understand each scholar's strengths. However, at the identical time, it would come up with a higher feel of the collective strengths of the classroom.

Take into account that there's no unmarried "proper" way to supply content material — however knowing your students' strengths can at the least assist you to method training extra thoughtfully, and to layout sports that scholars will love.

- It's culturally responsive

Pupil demographics have become an increasing number of various, and that's an awesome aspect. Variety creates a tradition of more than one view and enables students to learn how to work in teams to provide outcomes. At the identical time, if the classroom isn't always culturally responsive, then students won't experience welcome, and the blessings of a diverse classroom will no longer be found out. A culturally responsive lecture room may be identified thru intentionally taking an inclusive method, relating material to students' lives, and developing meaningful assignments.

Asset-primarily based coaching redirects the emphasis to the positives inherent inside the differences between college students. rather than wondering why some college students aren't picking up at the English language in addition to their peers or are talking with their friends in a different language than is used in the schoolroom, consider how fluency in their first language can assist them to learn English. If it's far easier for them to use computers set in an extraordinary language or to jot down their native language first, that can genuinely be a strength.

• It facilitates you get to understand your college students better

An instructor who takes an asset-primarily based view of their students should get to know their college students. Now and again, deficits and belongings seem inside the route of a school day. However, to absolutely recognize the assets of a scholar requires knowing who they are, what they prefer, and what they do.

The fine way to do that is to honestly have conversations with the students. These conversations can take place before the start of the day, during a break, or for the duration of unbiased learning time. College students revel in sharing matters about themselves and feeling like their teacher cares approximately them.

• It attracts college students' hobbies

A herbal final result of gaining knowledge of your college students better is that you'll learn more approximately their hobbies. And perhaps you can locate methods to relate those pursuits to the content you educate. Has there been a time whilst the equal well-known might be met but the content material used could be selected by using the scholars? For example, in a lesson on density, students ought to convey certain objects from home to test. That is a clean manner to carry within the pursuits of college students. To increase scholar engagement even extra, you could also base your elegance initiatives on student pastimes. This may bring content to lifestyles and stop all of the questions on why students should analyze this!

• It allows you to create student-targeted school rooms

In a simply pupil-focused lecture room, scholar voices need to be front and center. This will seem horrifying as it means you'll need to give up a sure level of control as an instructor. However, students can and will learn information on their very own. We're no longer the only owners of facts and expertise. College students need to sense as though the lecture room is their playground, where they can discover ways to assume, collaborate, and create statistics.

For a teacher to give up some manipulate within the lecture room and empower students to approach that they ought to trust that students deliver top-notch prices. It creates surroundings where students experience like they have got a voice and feature possession of their getting to know. A tremendous instance of that is letting students select their very own topics and doing their very own studies as opposed to preselecting the subjects for the students. If they pick a topic that isn't right for the task, then you may have a verbal exchange and see what else they might want to study.

• It connects to the earlier understanding

The maximum significant mastering takes place when it builds on what we already know. As teachers, we don't have any concept of what college students will take away from a lesson. We have learning goals, requirements to satisfy, and tests to a degree. This doesn't ensure that scholars analyze from a lesson exactly what we want them to examine. Instead, they may make their personal meaning.

Frequently, this means is connected to any earlier expertise the student may have. With an asset-based totally view of college students, any earlier know-how they convey into the mastering surroundings is a precious place to begin.

Asset-based coaching need to certainly reduce any lecture room conduct problems due to the fact relationships are built, and students are pictured as an entire character. You may probably nevertheless come across situations or college students who generally tend to motive disruptions inside the lecture room. Even if a scholar wishes to be disciplined or lose privileges, an average asset-primarily based view of the scholars means that these poor repercussions will sense much less punitive. College students will understand that they may be a vital part of the classroom and that their instructor enjoys having them.

Connecting to general discipline philosophies

The shift faraway from zero tolerance to restorative justice aligns nicely with asset-based totally teaching. College students are not handed out punishments that align with deficit-targeted teaching. Alternatively, they're brought in as companions within the subject technology and are given a voice. In each model, the strength shifts in the lecture room to create a community of learners.

Benefits for college students

College can be a very disturbing time for college kids.

Every so often, they talk totally distinctive languages at domestic or maybe they love playing video games that aren't allowed in college. Students will sense peer pressure to act and act in sure methods. They may be seeking to navigate social circles even at an equal time studying and acting inside the schoolroom. Asset-primarily based teaching facilitates college students to feel welcomed, supported, and valued. They are not numbers to train, assessments to grade, or commencement marks; they may be human beings who have a couple of identities, intersections, experiences, and backgrounds. Schoolroom behavior will improve as students are empowered and treated with positivity and respect. Focusing on strengths even whilst you are frustrated or challenged is not easy, but it'll pay dividends ultimately.

Five approaches to building an Asset-primarily based attitude in schooling

International training stories are too frequently advanced on a basis of deficit thinking, mainly inside the most evolved elements of the arena. at the same time as many worldwide educators are aware of the hassle and running difficult to opposite it, examples nonetheless abound global partnerships that continually lead to fundraisers, the belief that school rooms within the growing international should be in the back of the evolved global academically, network carrier experiences that feed savior complexes as opposed to undoing them, and the very use of phrases like "developed" vs. "developing," which means that one is in the back of the other. Even the shortage of a common language between lecture rooms is every so often perceived as a problem more than a gift, even by well-intentioned educators, because it makes communication extra complicated. Maximum of these mistakes originate in deeply ingrained and often unconscious biases that come from records of colonization and exploration that objectified, exploited, and stole from cultures being "observed."

Global schooling should not exacerbate strength differences, and plenty of worldwide educators work to opposite the paradigm by way of constructing partnerships founded in a "getting to know from and with" mentality, in which all partners bring identical if the unique, value to the table. While teachers work to create partnerships with the usage of such asset-based questioning, they can create collaborative relationships that work to undo our colonial beyond and establish new paradigms for worldwide gaining knowledge of. Following are a few key techniques that can assist.

1. Construct the connection along with your accomplice's study room on a foundation of mutual benefit, recognition, and energy.

All of the guidelines underneath play into this maximum essential of equity factors: worldwide educators who want opposite dominance paradigms attempt to make sure that each planning and mastering processes emphasize consistent and equitable collaboration. They strive to honor all voices, all views, and all reviews, to usually anticipate the pleasant intentions, and to continually "share the nicely," a word used at Mount Vernon Presbyterian School in Atlanta to suggest that educators have to always percentage electricity, time, and resources.

2. Throughout planning and mastering reviews, begin with questions as opposed to assertions and search for points of

intersection.

All instructors have desires and needs, and the maximum equitable partnerships meet the curricular wishes of all instructors involved. That does not necessarily mean that each teacher should be coaching the equal fabric to the same age companies; they could proportion content material, they might proportion age organizations, or they'll have neither in not unusual. What makes their partnerships a success is their potential to ask every different probing question, to discover each other's ideas, and to see their curricula as a Venn diagram, looking for factors of intersection that advantage both school rooms.

3. Get college students involved in spotting deficit mindsets when they emerge, and in strategizing approaches to flip the paradigm.

We regularly underestimate the position that scholars would possibly play in ensuring fairness in our lecture rooms. Global educators striving for equity can interact with their college students inside the effort to think seriously about authentic demanding situations in actual time through global partnerships, getting them worried in figuring out the ability caution symptoms of a deficit mindset. Once students have been worried about organizing the criterion for fairness, they may become a tremendous filter for everything that takes place inside the lecture room. My college students had been the first to point it out after I made deficit-primarily based assumptions in my own study room—and all of us discovered an extraordinary deal from our collective effort to define and make certain equity in our interactions with each different and the arena.

4. Lean into soreness whilst inequities emerge or

partnerships end up debatable.

I accept as true with it is an inherently human instinct to lean far away from pain and controversy, though that tendency can vary alongside cultural strains to some extent. we can most effectively resolve what we interact with; we can handiest make certain an extra just and peaceful world if we lean into controversy and tough conversations, if we emerge as secure with discomfort and deliberately engage in the hard work that equity and social justice require. I should best study from my college students by being open to their correcting me. Likewise, we can best turn the paradigm if we will let ourselves certainly hear and try and recognize perspectives, grounded in real reports, which vary from our own. Preserving it easy method we flow on the surface, missing the possibility to dig into the deeper complexities of the human enjoy.

5. Watch out for orienting answers toward solving problems to your partners; instead, build partnerships wherein students resolve for the world they realize and learn from the sector they don't.

As a writing instructor, I usually advised my college students that they should write what they knew, emphasizing that their personal story was the only one that changed into maximum authentically theirs to tell, whereas to tell the testimonies of others to require massive research and even then maybe rife with misrepresentation or generalization. In global development, the "solve-for" mentality has birthed many unsustainable and inappropriate solutions, all because one institution assumed they knew better than the alternative. Equitable international schooling strives to foster alternate makers and trouble solvers who recognize that mastering from and with leads us all to better answers in our own communities.

In international partnerships based on equitable action, college students examine from and with each different, however, the solutions they construct are for demanding situations of their very own groups, informed with the aid of what they discovered from their companions. within the nice examples of global partnerships, college students all around the globe work on the identical challenge because it manifests of their very own backyards, and they collaborate so that their moves carry collectively a couple of perspectives and reports, which lead to sustainable, multilateral development. This also creates an essential possibility for nearby partnerships which can help humanize worldwide challenges, ensuring that students apprehend the connections among global issues and nearby realities—and making summary standards like poverty extra concrete for more youthful rookies. Such partnerships additionally help college students recognize alternate makers and leaders in their very own communities, giving them the possibilities to participate in real, meaningful motion alongside individuals and groups running on the same troubles being addressed inside the college students' college or program. As Canadian anthropologist and country-wide Geographic creator, Wade Davis positioned it, "other cultures aren't a failed try to be you." If we can help our college students recognize this through worldwide partnerships that without a doubt equip them to collaborate on equal footing with their international counterparts, maybe they can start to see different cultures as the gift we so urgently want.

Fostering an asset-primarily based teaching attitude

They are saying that if we educators embrace the belongings our students carry, then our college students can shine more brightly and upward thrust to better stages of achievement. Let's think about that. The phrase "assets primarily based" is thrown around quite a chunk lately. But what does it clearly suggest to tackle an assets-based totally teaching mentality? What does that look like in our lecture rooms and our lesson plans? How does it sound? How does it affect the younger humans in our care?

Understanding our students

I suggest absolutely knowing them past the everlasting record folder. Sure, we want to recognize their academic history, their grades, their attendance, and their check scores, but there's so much greater. We need to recognize THEM. Who they are out of doors of the walls of our schoolhouse? What do they love? What makes them glad or sad? What do they pass domestic to? Who do they cross domestic to? Wherein did they come from? What traditions do they cost? What beliefs do they hold? One of the quality approaches to get to realize our students is through conversations. My favorite conversations with children passed off at some stage in reading or writing conferences. College students commonly in no way found out that I used to be filling wishes with one deed at some stage in our analyzing or writing conferences. However, I used to be.

I'd pull up a chair next to a scholar and simply have casual communication. My conversations were short, intentional, and effective. I found out approximately every scholar each for my part and academically. The conversations had a brought bonus. They helped us build relationships. My college students felt that I surely cared about them.

Valuing what our students deliver whilst we value what our college students convey, we apprehend their history and expertise and use it as a basis for their future studying. We take what we understand about them and leverage it in our classrooms to propel their increase and progress in language and content material. We help students understand that what they currently come to us with is helping them get smarter.

Valuing what our college students carry can occur obviously, or we might work on it. It'd need to be an intentional push on our behalf. As an instance, if we understand our college students communicate in any other language, gaining knowledge of a few keywords or phrases of their native language suggests that we price their local language. This additionally indicates the rest of the magnificence that understanding every other language is cool, that languages are exact, and that range is a nice element. For students who might be at the early degrees of language acquisition, imparting a few domestic language support values what they realize and prepares them for his or her goal language. Our local languages are belongings to us when we are obtaining a brand new language. In fact, I'd argue that the native language is the biggest asset.

Our children need to apprehend this strength and include it! So a lot of our college students don't realize this and as an alternative attempt to shed their native language because of embarrassment. This harms them not only personally however academically. There are many approaches to implement native language helps. One is to provide students with bilingual dictionaries or Google translate. Any other is to offer students facts and textual content of their local language. Encouraging and embracing local language support is a vital exercise. Faucet into your college students' families. Lots of our students come from culturally rich backgrounds which can be one-of-a-kind from our own. We can capitalize on this using commencing our school room doors and permitting parents to come in and share their expertise. If we invest time in studying our college students' households, we will understand what types of specialties they've or experiences they could share. Attain out to mother and father and invite them to return and present to the classroom.

One year, I had a pupil whose discern become a medical doctor in her domestic us of a. whilst we began gaining knowledge of about the frame systems, I invited the discern to come back percentage with the elegance. At the start, she turned reluctant. She feared her accent might no longer be understood by using the students. But I recommended her and fortunately she came. She brought medical artifacts and books and shared them with elegance. My students were so engaged and requested many questions. For weeks after she left, the students referred returned to her visit and what they discovered. It changed into actual and relevant. And I couldn't have taught it the manner she did with the actual-lifestyles stories she had.

Empowering voices

Our students want to be heard, and they crave it. It's our activity and obligation to extend their voices inside and outside of our school rooms. We can supply them the energy with the aid of providing many opportunities to percentage output. It's not crucial or legitimate for us to educate our students on a bunch of records. Facts are effortlessly forgotten and without the difficulty of Google. We're here to train them to think and analyze.

Whilst our school rooms are warm, safe environments for students, then they experience a welcome to take risks. For lots of college students, it isn't the fear of making a mistake that forestalls them from sharing, it's the fear of being embarrassed in front of their peers. This is especially proper for children inside the middle grades. Building a network that empowers voices within the classroom can take on much paperwork. Building in less teacher communication and greater pupil conversation in classes supports scholar's voice. One of my favored methods to try this is through cooperative agencies and based conversations including QSSSA and Socratic Circles. Similar to having students proportion orally in elegance, we will empower college students' voices through growing opportunities for them to proportion past the classroom walls. Students can percentage thru running a blog and other online alternatives. With the use of generation, our students can share their voices with the world.

Chapter Ten

Depression and Learning

Despair is a mental fitness illness. It has some genetic, organic, and environmental causes. It contributes to several different mental and bodily fitness troubles which include getting to knowability. It's far contamination that influences how someone feels, thinks, and acts. It is exclusive from everyday emotions of sadness or grief. Someone who has depression may also have much less strength. She or he may also become bored in daily sports and may sense unhappiness and grouchy for a long term, and it impacts men and women of all ages and backgrounds.
Melancholy is one of the emotional troubles, and hopelessness and helplessness are its important reasons. Depression is a commonplace hassle amongst university college students internationally and it affects a students' ability to carry out sports of the day-by-day lifestyles. Despair is marked via unhappy feelings amongst college students that are known as a not unusual intellectual illness." countrywide Institute of intellectual fitness located that during their college lifestyles many college students enjoy the first signs and symptoms of despair. Depressed college students frequently feel unhappy and discounts in educational overall performance. Untreated melancholy generally interferes in day-these days' activities and lasts for a long time. Depressed human beings forget about their

very own successes and desirable tendencies while exaggerating their faults and disasters. Student's educational overall performance which each individual should carry out in all cultures has emerged as a crucial purpose of the academic method. Student's personality, education, motivation, mental health, and training also impact instructional performance. College life can be known as a widespread transition duration, where college students enjoy many stuff the first time, in, as an example new way of life, exposure to new cultures, friends, roommates, unique methods of wondering, and also deal with a unique amount of pressure.

First years in university may be a very demanding time for lots of students. Whilst students cannot control those new first studies, they emerge as depressed. There are terrible consequences of depression on pupil achievement. Scholar's success is negatively related to despair, and depressed college students uncovered lower average factors and spend minimal time on homework. So the existing look at changed into designed to decide the results of despair on pupil's instructional overall performance at twelfth grade. Following goals are stored for the look at. 1. To measure the level of the melancholy of intermediate college students. 2. To perceive the instructional overall performance of the scholars at an intermediate degree. 3. To measure the consequences of despair on college students' academic performance. The following hypotheses are formulated and tested: The research hypotheses are as follows; 1. there is a poor impact of melancholy on pupil's instructional overall performance. 2. There may be significant differences among the instructional performance of college students having low, medium, and high stage despair. The above hypotheses had been tested thru null hypotheses. 1. There is no impact of depression on student's educational performance. 2. There is no significant difference between the educational performance of college students having low, medium, and high degree depression.

Despair is defined as a psychiatric ailment and the not unusual intellectual illness of gift century that is referred to as psychiatric cold. It has terrible consequences on our behaviors including loss of interest, productivity, and social contact. the eleventh leading purpose of dying is suicide in USA Suicide, which takes place about every sixteen minutes and Psychiatric diseases have been identified at the time in their dying in nearly all of the individuals who devote suicide. Through high-quality mood, we feel true, which has wonderful effects and inspires us to do what we wish. Whilst a little one is separated from a number one attachment parent, as within the Harlow research of rhesus monkeys, the result is not typically despair and passivity, the immune system also gets damage, which leads closer to depressive illness. Records of separations, rejections, and insecure attachments can be related to depressed human beings. As we stated in advance, however, humans with a history of glad and comfortable attachments may additionally fall into prolonged depression due to the loss of a loved lifelong associate. Whilst depressed and non-depressed humans requested to consider happier times, non-depressed people cheer up. However depressed people sense even worse, as though the satisfying memory makes them experience that they'll by no means be glad once more. Depressed humans showcase a negatively explanatory style than non-depressive people. Depression is related to a negative, pessimistic way of explaining and decoding failure. Careworn prompted terrible emotions may have various results on health. This is especially up to now depressed or anger susceptible

Many humans, and once in a while their households, feel embarrassed or ashamed about having despair. But it isn't a signal of a personal weak point. It's not a character flaw. Someone who is depressed isn't "loopy," melancholy is a clinical illness. It's due to adjustments inside the herbal chemical compounds in the brain. Maximum professionals consider that an aggregate of the circle of relatives records (someone's genes) and worrying lifestyles activities can cause depression.

Fitness troubles might also reason depression or make it worse. It's commonplace for people with lengthy-time period (persistent) fitness troubles like coronary artery disease, diabetes, cancer, or continual ache to sense depression. It is essential to recognize that depression may be treated. Step one towards feeling higher is often just due to the fact the trouble exists.

What are the signs?

The signs and symptoms of melancholy may be hard to be aware of at the start. They vary among people, and it's clean to confuse them with simply feeling "off." the two most common signs and symptoms are:

• Feeling sad or hopeless almost every day for at least two weeks.

• Dropping hobby in or not getting pleasure from most sports that were once fun, and feeling this manner nearly every day for at the least two weeks.

Different signs and symptoms may seem. A person with

despair might also, almost every day:

- Consume or sleep more or much less than common.
- Sense worn-out.
- Experience is unworthy or guilty.
- Locate it hard to cognizance, don't forget things, or make decisions.

A severe symptom of despair is thinking about demise or suicide. In case you or someone you care approximately talks approximately this or about feeling hopeless, get help right away.

How is it dealt with?

Medical doctors generally treat depression with medicines or counseling. Frequently a combination of the two works exceptional. Many people don't get assistance because they think that they will recover from the melancholy on their own. But some humans do no longer get better without remedy. Antidepressant medicines can improve the signs and symptoms of melancholy in 1 to three weeks. But it can take six to eight weeks to look for more improvement. Your medical doctor will in all likelihood have you preserve taking these medicines for at least six months. In many instances, counseling can work in addition to medicines to deal with slight to moderate despair. Counseling is performed by way of licensed intellectual health vendors, such as psychologists and social workers.

If melancholy is due to a clinical problem, treating that trouble may additionally help relieve the depression. Depression is among the most treatable of intellectual problems. Among eighty percent and ninety percentage of people with despair finally, respond properly to treatment. Almost all patients benefit little comfort from their signs and symptoms. Earlier than an analysis or remedy, a health expert must behavior an intensive diagnostic evaluation, inclusive of an interview and possibly a bodily exam. In a few cases, blood takes a look at is probably completed to ensure the despair isn't because of a clinical circumstance like thyroid trouble. The evaluation is to become aware of specific signs and symptoms, medical and circle of relatives records, cultural elements, and environmental factors to reach analysis and plan a direction of movement.

Medicine: mind chemistry can also contribute to a character's despair and may aspect into their remedy. For that reason, antidepressants are probably prescribed to help modify one's Mind chemistry. These medications are not sedatives, "uppers" or tranquilizers. They are no longer habit-forming. Commonly antidepressant medicinal drugs have no stimulating impact on human beings no longer experiencing depression.

Antidepressants can also produce a few improvements inside the first week or two of use. Complete blessings might not be seen for two to three months. If an affected person feels little or no improvement after several weeks, his or her psychiatrist can modify the dose of the medicine or add or substitute another antidepressant. In some conditions, different psychotropic medicinal drugs can be beneficial. It's crucial to allow your medical doctor to know if a remedy does not work or if you experience aspect results.

Psychiatrists normally recommend that patients retain to take the medicinal drug for six or more months after signs have stepped forward. Longer-term maintenance remedies can be counseled to decrease the chance of destiny episodes for certain people in excessive danger. Psychotherapy: Psychotherapy, or "talk therapy," is on occasion used on my own for treatment of slight despair; for moderate to extreme depression, psychotherapy is regularly used together with antidepressant medicines. Cognitive-behavioral remedy (CBT) has been determined to be powerful in treating despair. CBT is a shape of therapy focused on the prevailing and problem fixing. CBT facilitates a person to apprehend distorted wondering and then trade behaviors and wondering.

Psychotherapy can also involve most effective the man or woman, but it can consist of others. For example, family or couples therapy can assist deal with problems inside those near relationships. Organization remedy involves human beings with comparable illnesses.

Depending on the severity of the depression, the remedy can take a few weeks or plenty longer. In many cases, giant development can be made in ten to fifteen sessions.

Electroconvulsive remedy (ECT) is a clinical treatment most normally used for sufferers with intense important depression or bipolar ailment who have no longer replied to different treatments. It involves a short electric stimulation of the mind while the affected person is below anesthesia. An affected person commonly gets ECT two to three instances per week for a complete of six to twelve remedies. ECT has been used since the Forties, and lots of years of studies have caused essential upgrades. Additionally, it is controlled using a team of skilled scientific specialists inclusive of a psychiatrist, an anesthesiologist, and a nurse or health practitioner assistant.

What are you able to do to help someone with despair?

If a person you care approximately is depressed, you could sense helplessness. But there are some things you may do.

• Help the character get treatment or live with it. This is the fine aspect you may do.

• Aid and encourage the character.

• Help the individual have suitable health conduct. Urge him or her to get normal exercising, consume a balanced weight loss program, and get sufficient sleep.

• Contend with yourself. Ask others to present you emotional and realistic guide even as you are supporting a pal or cherished person who has melancholy.

• Hold the range for a suicide disaster center on or close to your telephone. To find a suicide prevention crisis center in your province, go to the Canadian affiliation for Suicide Prevention website at http://suicideprevention.ca/need-assist. If you or someone you realize talks approximately suicide or feeling hopeless, get assistance proper away.

How Does despair without delay affect studying?
People with melancholy may be unable to finish obligations that require an excessive motor and cognitive competencies. They will experience stress, scatterbrained, overwhelmed, or without difficulty pissed off. Even fundamental regular tasks come to be hard. Despair impairs cognitive functioning. This intellectual fitness trouble interferes with wholesome concept approaches and influences someone's capacity to concentrate and make choices. It changes the brain, and lots of humans with depression discover they regularly experience reminiscence issues and feature hassle remembering activities or information.

Different signs and symptoms of despair contribute to getting to know problems. Despair can depart some individuals feeling irritable, agitated, hectic, and not able to focus. Others discover they're no longer interested in pursuits, sports, or studying new matters. Temper swings make it difficult to pay attention, even as feelings of hopelessness or low vanity can purpose individuals to trust they shouldn't bother or virtually can't study new matters. Melancholy also affects sleep, and insomnia and hypersomnia can in addition impact intellectual health and feature. When you think about scientific melancholy, you possibly think about feeling unhappy and down for lengthy intervals of time; dropping your energy and your interest in belongings you used to enjoy; dozing too much or too little, or eating too much or too little. However, except those, depression can clearly trade your potential to think. It could impair your interest and memory, as well as your facts processing and selection-making abilities. It could also decrease your cognitive flexibility (the potential to evolve your dreams and techniques to changing situations) and executive functioning (the ability to take all of the steps to get something executed).

For people with intense melancholy, medicinal drugs can offer some relief of low temper and electricity, bolster the motivation to engage in fun and vital activities, and help people return to regular snoozing and consuming patterns. However, we don't understand whether or not antidepressant medicines treat cognitive impairment related to depression. Recently, a worldwide studies crew tried to answer this query as a part of a larger look at depression treatment. To study the impact of three commonplace antidepressant medications on depression-related cognitive impairment, the researchers requested over one thousand humans with depression who had been taking both escitalopram (Lexapro), sertraline (Zoloft), or venlafaxine-XR (Effexor-XR) to undergo sizeable cognitive trying out. In short, not one of the medications helped. Of these sufferers, ninety-five percent showed no improvement on any of the cognitive impairments mentioned above, and none of the three capsules was higher than the others at improving cognitive signs and symptoms.

This result isn't always completely sudden, antidepressant medications are mainly intended to assist enhance temper and boom the capability to participate in useful and enjoyable activities, two key components of melancholy remedy. It's additionally well worth noting that one-of-a-kind components and strategies of the mind are responsible for cognitive (versus emotional) functioning; this could explain why the three pills examined didn't seem to assist enhance cognitive signs and symptoms. New tablets for despair can be capable of address those signs and symptoms as nicely. Past medications, the problem-fixing remedies can train human beings the way to enhance their hassle-solving skills, and cognitive-behavioral remedies can teach people to recognize and mission distorted questioning patterns. Every other method, cognitive remediation therapy, makes use of exercise drills to improve memory and government functioning. Combining these behavioral interventions with antidepressants may also yield higher outcomes for enhancing melancholy-related cognitive impairments.

There are a few obstacles to this examination: it's not known if the participants had cognitive impairments before they advanced melancholy, and the period of drug remedy and observe-up turned into quick; eight weeks overall. However, this examination is vital because the cognitive impairment symptoms of despair have acquired little attention and haven't always been the target of medications for depression. It shows that we have an extended manner to move in supporting people with depression to go back to an everyday stage of full intellectual functioning.

Depression signs can range from mild to severe and can include:
- Feeling sad or having a depressed mood
- Loss of interest or satisfaction in sports as soon as enjoyed
- Adjustments in urge for food — weight reduction or benefit unrelated to weight-reduction plan
- Trouble dozing or napping too much
- Lack of strength or extended fatigue
- Increase in purposeless bodily pastime (e.g., hand-wringing or pacing) or slowed moves and speech (actions observable with the aid of others)
- Feeling nugatory or guilty
- Problem thinking, concentrating, or making choices
- Mind of dying or suicide

Symptoms need to last a minimum of weeks for a prognosis of despair. Additionally, medical conditions (e.g., thyroid problems, a brain tumor, or vitamin deficiency) can mimic signs of depression so it's far critical to rule out popular clinical reasons. Despair affects an expected one in fifteen adults (6.7%) in any given twelve months. And one in six human beings (16.6%) will experience melancholy at a while in their life. melancholy can strike at any time, but on common, first appears at some point of the past due to teens to mid-twenties. Girls are more likely than men to experience melancholy. a few studies show that one-third of girls will revel in a major depressive episode in their lifetime

.

Despair isn't the same as sadness or Grief/Bereavement

The demise of a loved one, lack of an activity, or the ending of a relationship are tough experiences for someone to undergo. It is regular for emotions of disappointment or grief to increase in response to such conditions. The ones experiencing loss often might describe themselves as being "depressed." But being sad isn't always the same as having despair. The grieving procedure is herbal and unique to every man or woman and shares some of the identical capabilities of despair. Both grief and depression may additionally contain severe unhappiness and withdrawal from standard sports. They're also different in crucial approaches:

• In grief, painful emotions are available waves, frequently intermixed with advantageous recollections of the deceased. In predominant melancholy, temper and/or hobby (satisfaction) are decreased for most of the weeks.

• In grief, self-esteem is usually maintained. In essential despair, emotions of worthlessness and self-loathing are not unusual.

• For a few human beings, the dying of a cherished you'll be able to bring forth the most important depression. Losing an activity or being a sufferer of a bodily attack or a primary disaster can lead to despair for a few humans.

Whilst grief and despair co-exist, the grief is greater intense and lasts longer than grief without despair. Notwithstanding some overlap among grief and melancholy, they are one of a kind. Distinguishing between them can assist humans to get the help, assist or remedy they want.

Risk elements for melancholy

Melancholy can affect anybody—even someone who seems to stay in enormously ideal circumstances.

•   Biochemistry: differences in positive chemical substances within the brain may additionally make contributions to signs of melancholy.

•   Genetics: depression can run in families. As an instance, if one equal twin has depression, the opposite has a seventy percent hazard of having the infection sometimes in life.

•   Personality: people with low self-esteem, who are without problems crushed via strain, or who're commonly pessimistic appear to be more likely to enjoy melancholy.

•   Environmental elements: non-stop publicity to violence, overlook, abuse or poverty may additionally make a few people more at risk of melancholy.

Depression can impair one's cognitive functioning. The sickness interferes with one's idea system, the capability to make selections, and concentration. Despair adjustments the mind, which can slow the mind's functioning. Depressed human beings frequently revel in reminiscence problems and feature problems remembering occasions or information. As a result, they may be unable to complete duties that require both high-motor and cognitive abilities. Patients may additionally seem burdened, scatterbrained, overwhelmed, or grow to be annoyed without problems. Even everyday obligations may be tough for a person struggling with despair. Those intellectual impairments are especially high-priced to kids and college students who're still attempting to analyze essential skills.

While you're depressed, you aren't the nice model of yourself. You may be feeling unhappiness, hopelessness, or depression, but these aren't the simplest symptoms of depression. Depression can cause alcoholism and suicide, but there's one lesser-regarded symptom of despair that human beings live with every day. Depression doesn't simply get within the manner of being satisfied. It can additionally interrupt your capability to suppose. It hampers your interest, reminiscence, and selection-making capabilities. You can discover that your government features are restrained so that you start having hassle seeing your way through problems. Depression generally stems from an interruption or reduction of the brain's chemical messengers. Those interruptions may also impair your cognitive skills.

Many individuals who be afflicted by melancholy may also be recognized with any other mental fitness ailment, along with attention deficit disease (upload). In addition, humans with melancholy are also much more likely to enjoy attention problems. Researchers don't but recognize precisely what causes attention troubles in humans with melancholy, but there may be a correlation between the two. Both human beings with unipolar and bipolar melancholy enjoy awareness issues, no matter age. It's also worth citing that a few antidepressant medications may also have cognitive side effects. In case you suffer from despair-associated attention problems, you may have hassle focusing on one venture long enough to finish it. If you observe a surprising onset of interest troubles, speak to your physician. There's a threat your interest troubles might also stem from despair or any other medical trouble. If you're stricken by despair, you can additionally have trouble with reminiscence loss. It's a fairly common symptom of despair, so recognize which you're now not suffering on your own. In 2013, researchers located that humans with melancholy had problems identifying items that had been equal or similar to objects that they had just seen. 2015 have a look posted in Cognition & Emotion also concluded that despair may additionally motive short-term memory loss. While you're experiencing depression-related memory loss, you can don't forget what you ate for breakfast, or you can forget the details of a tremendous occasion. Remember that there are numerous different reasons for reminiscence loss, so communicate with your medical doctor about your signs.

Government characteristic

Despair can also affect your government function, which affects your ability to system records. Government feature is regularly referred to as the CEO of the mind because it's in the rate of getting matters performed. Government characteristic impairments might also get in the manner of easy responsibilities like paying payments or remembering to go back a smartphone name. This crucial mind function helps us control time, shift consciousness, plan and organize, and don't forget vital details. Government function issues are often acute and can be much more likely to occur whilst a person is distinctly stressed, sad, or sleep-deprived. Luckily, anybody can improve their government characteristic at any time with instructional techniques and behavioral approaches. If you're experiencing troubles with government characteristics, attempt breaking massive duties down into smaller chunks, create to-do lists, and evaluate them regularly.

Decision-making

Because melancholy impairs your potential to make choices, you could have trouble making even minor decisions like where to go for dinner. Professionals often help patients' combat indecision with treatment options like cognitive behavioral therapy (CBT). Those treatments help sufferers analyze picks and spot all of the viable effects. People who suffer from melancholy-associated indecision can also make their lives less complicated by restricting the wide variety of selections they must make. As an instance, they will have the same element for breakfast each morning or take the same course to work each day.

The way to treat melancholy-related cognitive impairment

It's crucial to remember that the cognitive impairment, in this situation, is a symptom of another condition. There are brief-time period answers to treating and living with cognitive impairment, but the first-class long-time period solution is to treat the despair itself. Depression may be dealt with with remedy and/or medication. Selective serotonin reuptake inhibitors (SSRIs) can also help alleviate melancholy-associated cognitive impairment. Within an identical manner, treating despair with medicinal drug-loose remedies may have an equal effect over a more prolonged time frame. The best news about this symptom is that cognitive features may return after the despair is lifted. NeuroscienceNews.com picture is in the public domain. At some stage in melancholy remedy, the hassle-solving remedy can teach human beings the way to solve problems. CBT can educate people to recognize and cope with any distorted questioning styles. And cognitive remediation therapy uses exercise drills to assist enhance government characteristics and memory. These types of remedies can be used on their very own or in conjunction with medication to yield better consequences.